Math

as a Way of Knowing

SUSAN OHANIAN

Stenhouse Publishers

The Galef Institute

Strategies for Teaching and Learning Professional Library

Administrators: Supporting School Change by Robert Wortman
Assessment: Continuous Learning by Lois Bridges
Creating Your Classroom Community by Lois Bridges
Drama as a Way of Knowing by Paul G. Heller
Math as a Way of Knowing by Susan Ohanian
Music as a Way of Knowing by Nick Page

Look for announcements of future titles in this series on dance, second language learners, literature, physical education, science, visual arts, and writing.

Stenhouse Publishers, 431 York Street, York, Maine 03909
The Galef Institute, 11050 Santa Monica Boulevard, Third Floor, Los Angeles, California 90025

Copyright © 1995 The Galef Institute.

Library of Congress Cataloging-in-Publication Data
Ohanian, Susan.
    Math as a way of knowing / Susan Ohanian.
       p.   cm. — (Strategies for teaching and learning professional library)
    Includes bibliographical references (p.).
    ISBN 1-57110-051-2 (alk. paper)
    1. Mathematics—Study and teaching (Elementary)   I. Title.
  II. Series.
  QA135.5.O34 1996
  372.7'044—dc20
                                            96-45740
                                           CIP

Manufactured in the United States of America on acid-free paper
01 00 99 98 97 96 8 7 6 5 4 3 2 1

Dear Colleague,

This is an exciting time for us to be educators.

Research across disciplines informs our understanding of human learning and development. We know how to support students as active, engaged learners in our classrooms. We know how to continuously assess student learning and development to make sensitive, instructional decisions. This is the art of teaching—knowing how to respond effectively at any given moment to our students' developmental needs.

As educators, we know that learning the art of teaching takes time, practice, and lots of professional support. To that end, the Strategies for Teaching and Learning Professional Library was developed. Each book invites you to explore theory (to know why) in the context of exciting teaching strategies (to know how) connected to evaluation of your students' learning as well as your own (to know you know). In addition, you'll find in-depth information about the unique rigors and challenges of each discipline, to help you make the most of the rich learning and teaching opportunities each discipline offers.

> Use the books' *Dialogues* on your own and in the study groups to reflect upon your practices. The Dialogues invite responses to self-evaluative questions, experimentation with new instructional strategies in classrooms, and perhaps a rethinking of learning philosophy and classroom practices stimulated by new knowledge and understanding.

> *Shoptalks* offer you lively reviews of the best and latest professional literature including professional journals and associations.

> *Teacher-To-Teacher Field Notes* are full of tips and experiences from practicing educators who offer different ways of thinking about teaching practices and a wide range of classroom strategies they've found practical and successful.

As you explore and reflect on teaching and learning, we believe you'll continue to refine and extend your teaching art, and enjoy your professional life and the learning lives of your students.

Here's to the art of teaching!

Lois Bridges
Professional Development Editorial Director,
The Galef Institute

The Strategies for Teaching and Learning Professional Library is part of the Galef Institute's school reform initiative *Different Ways of Knowing*.

Different Ways of Knowing is a philosophy of education based on research in child development, cognitive theory, and multiple intelligences. It offers teachers, administrators, specialists, and other school and district educators continuing professional growth opportunities integrated with teaching and learning materials. The materials are supportive of culturally and linguistically diverse school populations and help all teachers and children to be successful. Teaching strategies focus on interdisciplinary, thematic instruction integrating history and social studies with the performing and visual arts, literature, writing, math, and science. Developed with the leadership of Senior Author Linda Adelman, *Different Ways of Knowing* has been field tested in hundreds of classrooms across the country.

For more information, write or call

The Galef Institute
11050 Santa Monica Boulevard, Third Floor, Los Angeles, California 90025
Tel 310.479.8883
Fax 310.473.9720

Strategies for Teaching and Learning Professional Library

Contributors

President
Linda Adelman

Vice President Programs and Communications
Sue Beauregard

Professional Development Editorial Director
Lois Bridges

Editor
Resa Gabe Nikol

Editorial Assistants
Elizabeth Finison, Wendy Sallin

Designers
Melvin Harris, Delfina Marquez-Noé,
Sarah McCormick, Jennifer Swan Myers,
Julie Suh

Photographers
Ted Beauregard, Dana Ross

I would like to express my gratitude to the many teachers who invited me into their classrooms and to the students who inspire me still. —SO

Special thanks to Andrew G. Galef and Bronya Pereira Galef for their continuing commitment to our nation's children and educators.

Contents

Chapter 1
Mathematics as a Way of Doing

When teachers announce "math time," children across the country participate in active, hands-on exploration of mathematics concepts. In Tampa, Florida, when kindergartners are asked their favorite thing in school, they reply enthusiastically, "Graphs!" Primary graders at the Learning Center for the Deaf in Framingham, Massachusetts, get out their lunches and collect data on the three most popular sandwiches. On his own, a special education student in Muncie, Indiana, decides to collect data on the number of his classmates ordering chocolate milk vs. white milk. Elementary graders in Lincoln, California, collect data on family sizes; they learn how to summarize data and talk about what "typical" means.

Students learn the importance of writing in math class. In Irving, California, six year olds write their own math book about transforming a geometric shape; in Piedmont, California, seven year olds write math riddles. After a visit to the zoo, children in Milwaukee, Wisconsin, compare their heights with that of a giraffe, keeping records of the results. Children in Baton Rouge figure out how many of them it takes to equal the height of a *Tyrannosaurus rex*. After entering and studying the resulting figures on a wall chart, they write predictions for other dinosaurs. History takes on new meaning when primary graders in Milwaukee, Wisconsin, recreate the dimensions of the Mayflower on the playground—and then crowd the number of passengers into those dimensions. They talk and write about what those numbers mean.

Eight and nine year olds in Tucson figure out how many ways a candy manufacturer could package 36 candies. They write letters to the manufacturer explaining their recommendations for best candy box designs. In Belgrade, Montana, children in math club explain *Fibonacci* numbers to their parents—and write letters about their math activities to the Exxon Education Foundation, which helped get their club started. Children see how math is integrated with science by measuring animals at the zoo; how math is integrated with history as they count how many people could fit on the Mayflower; and how art is integrated with math by creating candy packaging.

Children learn that math is everywhere. In San Francisco, youngsters inspired by Margaret Mahy's provocative picture book, *17 Kings and 42 Elephants*, figure out how to share the elephants among the kings fairly and thereby "invent" division—with remainders. They keep track of the teeth their class loses; they take a poll on things that scare them; they research the waste discarded by their families and then figure out inventive ways to report their findings and to act upon them.

Mathematics is an active, ongoing way of perceiving and interacting with the world.

In looking at basic mathematics problems from many dimensions and in using a variety of plans and materials to solve these problems, children are developing a feeling for numbers, an ability to recognize patterns, and an awareness of mathematical relationships. They are learning to do math. For these children, mathematics is not just a series of facts and operations to be memorized; mathematics is an active, ongoing way of perceiving and interacting with the world.

Teachers are working to bring their classroom math practice more in line with the verbs outlined in the 1989 National Council of Teachers of Mathematics *Curriculum and Evaluation Standards for School Mathematics* (NCTM Standards)—to make sure that students are actively engaged in mathematical explorations.

DIALOGUE

What are ten verbs I would use to describe what students do during typical math lessons in my classroom?

1. _____   6. _____

2. _____   7. _____

3. _____   8. _____

4. _____   9. _____

5. _____   10. _____

DIALOGUE

Here are the verbs used in the NCTM publication *Curriculum and Evaluation Standards for School Mathematics.*

1. *investigate*
2. *explore*
3. *explain*
4. *describe*
5. *develop*
6. *invent*
7. *relate*
8. *model*
9. *apply*
10. *represent*

What surprises are there, if any, in the differences or similarities between the two sets of verbs?

_____

_____

What's Happened to Arithmetic?

Arithmetic has traditionally been taught with the assumption that there is sequence to presenting curriculum. We taught children to memorize a procedure which they practiced using paper and pencil. They had to memorize one simple procedure before going on to the next procedure, eventually moving on to more complex concepts. "Getting the basics" meant knowing the one right answer to a procedure. But as Lauren Resnick observes in *Education and Learning To Think* (1987), both research and classroom practice challenge the theory that children need long years of drilling on the basics before moving on to problem solving and thinking. Teachers and children alike are learning that all children can and should be honored as mathematical thinkers.

This means we have to look at both students and mathematics in new ways, at all grade levels. In the preface to *Mathematics: A Human Endeavor* (1982) by Harold R. Jacobs, Martin Gardner gives us a glimpse of what this means. Gardner tells of a high-school algebra student who, during a study period, began analyzing a game of tick-tack-toe. The teacher reprimanded him for "fooling around." Gardner points out that this teacher was wrong, that tick-tack-toe is an excellent way of introducing such concepts as set theory, group symmetry, probability, game theory, n-dimensional geometry, topology, and abstract algebra.

In the mathematics classroom of today, children are encouraged to see math throughout their day. They are encouraged to think like mathematicians, which means finding patterns in numbers as well as playing with the possibilities of mathematics. Thinking like mathematicians means solving problems in a variety of ways, using a variety of tools and procedures.

Algebra and geometry are no longer topics reserved for college-bound students in high school. One of the tenets of the NCTM is "algebra for all." And the place this starts is kindergarten.

Just as teachers don't hold off introducing children to good literature until they are in high school, so, too, do children need "good" math problems from the first day of school. As Grant Wiggins observes in *Assessing Student Performance* (1994), "younger students will never make it to the upper levels of academe without being repeatedly confronted with the most important questions and perspectives on those questions, beginning at the earliest levels of education."

DIALOGUE

List five occasions in the last month—outside of school—in which you have used arithmetic.

1. _____

2. _____

3. _____

4. _____

5. _____

Now go back and note what you used to solve each problem: paper and pencil, calculator, mental math, estimation. Also indicate whether you made sure you had an exact answer or if you were satisfied with an approximation.

Math for the Future

The NCTM Standards set goals for reforming K-12 mathematics instruction. The goals provide a vision of what it means to be mathematically competent in today's world.

The NCTM Standards have been acclaimed by an impressive variety of individuals and groups, including the U.S. Secretary of Education, the Institute of Electrical and Electronics Engineers, the American Association of Retired Persons, the American Association of University Women, and the American Bankers Association.

All students can develop the confidence, knowledge, and techniques for using math to solve everyday problems.

Three assumptions have shaped the vision set forth in the NCTM Standards.

Mathematics is something that a person does. To learn math, students must be engaged in exploring, conjecturing, and thinking—learning from the experience of doing.

Mathematics has broad content encompassing many fields. From the early grades onward, students can benefit from exposures that reveal the usefulness of math.

Mathematical power can—and must—be at the command of all students in a technological society. All students can develop the confidence, knowledge, and techniques for using math to solve everyday problems.

Five learning goals form the foundation for the Standards. Students should be able to

- value mathematics
- reason mathematically
- communicate mathematically
- become confident of their mathematical abilities
- become mathematical problem solvers.

To achieve these goals, the Standards recommend that teachers in early grades place more emphasis on number sense and less on complex paper-and-pencil figuring; more on children learning to work together and less on rote memorization of rules; and more on talking and writing about their problem-solving strategies and less on single-answer, one-method problems.

SHOPTALK

For additional information about the NCTM *Curriculum and Evaluation Standards for School Mathematics*, contact

Communications Coordinator
National Council of Teachers of Mathematics
1906 Association Drive
Reston, Virginia 22091

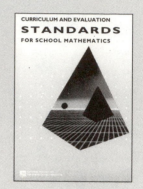

CURRICULUM AND EVALUATION
STANDARDS
FOR SCHOOL MATHEMATICS

Primary-grade students should work on real-world problems involving estimation, number sense, computation, geometry and spatial reasoning, measurement, statistics and probability, fractions, decimals, number patterns, and relationships.

Every classroom from kindergarten upwards should be stocked with a set of calculators. Computers also should be familiar tools for children.

Students should have ample opportunity to explore mathematical concepts with materials known as manipulatives. Popular examples include interlinking plastic cubes, geometric pattern blocks, two-color counters, and tangram puzzles (which help develop spatial reasoning). Such aids assist children in relating abstract ideas about numbers to objects they can see, touch, and manipulate.

Field Notes: Teacher-To-Teacher

I encourage my youngsters to teach each other. Nicole has the hang of it. She will bring her work around to each table so her classmates can take a look at what she did. I tell my students, "if you're having problems, ask Nicole for advice."

Penny Vincent
Ernest Stapleton School
Rio Rancho, New Mexico

Changing Structures for Classrooms and Curriculum

Three basic principles underlying the changing mathematics curriculum deal mostly with teaching techniques and to a lesser extent with mathematics content. Along with the NCTM Standards, leaders in mathematics education advocate

- heterogeneous grouping
- collaborative learning
- interdisciplinary studies.

Pointing out that in the real world most problems we encounter are not neatly set up for us the way they are in textbooks, the Standards underscore the importance of students finding mathematical problems in everyday situations and developing a variety of strategies to solve those problems. One of the most striking changes is that the Standards put the teacher of today in charge.

DIALOGUE

What is the first thing I think of when I remember math class in my own school days?

_____

_____

What is the first thing I think of when I contemplate my own math teaching?

_____

_____

Are my math class memories positive or negative? Why?

_____

_____

What if anything, do my two experiences have in common?

_____

_____

_____

New Ways of Looking at Children

Rather than grouping children into high math or low math, teachers are seeing that all children can engage in mathematical thinking. Children are intrigued by interesting and challenging problems. For example, when primary graders return to school from a visit to the zoo, they decide to compare their heights with the height of a giraffe. Before they try to get a numerical answer, they talk about the problem—in both large and small groups. They talk about problem-solving strategies as well as possible answers.

We are learning not to rely on textbooks but to explore mathematics in the world around us.

DIALOGUE

How high is the Empire State Building?

How might you solve this problem? Although you might well decide to look up the answer in the library, list three other strategies you might use.

_____

_____

_____

Write a statement about what you learned about yourself as a learner and about solving math problems.

_____

_____

New Ways of Looking at Math

Teachers and children are learning that mathematics is not a spectator sport. The NCTM Standards are helping us teach and learn mathematics in new ways; we are learning not to rely on textbooks but to explore mathematics in the world around us.

In *The Having of Wonderful Ideas and Other Essays on Teaching and Learning* (1987), Harvard researcher Eleanor Duckworth recounts the experience of seven-year-old Kevin who gets the idea of putting 10 drinking straws of different lengths into order by their length. She describes his joy in getting the idea of doing this and his pleasure in accomplishing his self-set task. In Duckworth's words, "The having of wonderful ideas is what I consider the essence of intellectual development. And I consider it the essence of pedagogy to give Kevin the occasion to have his wonderful ideas and to let him feel good about himself for having them."

In Lynn Zolli's classroom in San Francisco, all her eight and nine year olds tackle the same division problem; and in sharing their varying strategies, children learn to celebrate different ways of solving a problem.

As well as honoring different problem-solving strategies, children in this classroom work in groups and, in so doing, follow the advice of corporate America. This advice has been summarized in a booklet published by the U.S. Department of Labor, *What Work Requires of Schools: A SCANS Report for America 2000* (1991). The report lists "Workplace Know-Hows," the five competencies needed for solid job performance in the twenty-first century.

1. Resources—identifies, organizes, plans, and allocates resources
2. Interpersonal Skills—works with others
   a. Participates as a member of a team
   b. Teaches others new skills
   c. Serves clients/customers
   d. Exercises leadership
   e. Negotiates
   f. Works with diversity
3. Information—acquires and uses information; comfortable conveying information orally and in writing
4. Systems—understands complex interrelationships; understands own work in the context of the work of those around them; monitors and corrects own performance
5. Technology—works with a variety of technologies.

These students learn what adults come to know in the workplace; they learn that participating in a team helps them get the job done.

Characteristics of Today's and Tomorrow's Schools. The government report *What Work Requires of Schools: A SCANS Report for America 2000* also summarizes the characteristics of schools today and the characteristics that business and government leaders hope for in tomorrow's schools, shown in the chart on the following page.

	Schools of Today	Schools of Tomorrow
Strategy	• Focus on development of basic skills • Testing separate from teaching	• Focus on development of thinking skills • Assessment integral to teaching
Learning Environment	• Recitation and recall from short-term memory • Students work individually • Hierarchically sequenced—basics before higher order	• Students actively construct knowledge • Collaborative problem solving • Skills learned in the context of real problems
Management	• Supervision by administration	• Learner-centered, teacher-directed
Outcome	• Only some students learn to think	• All students learn to think

New Horizons in Math

In his introduction to *On the Shoulders of Giants: New Approaches to Numeracy* (1990), Lynn Arthur Steen points to visualization as "one of the most rapidly growing areas of mathematical and scientific research," noting that "the visual display of data to search for hidden patterns" is the first step in data analysis. From kindergartners in Tampa to six year olds in Las Cruces to nine year olds in Irving, children think data analysis is great. Across the country, anyone who enters primary-grade classrooms can see at a glance in which month most children were born, how many teeth they've lost, what color eyes they have, what type of shoes they're wearing, the type of pets they have, the type of pets they'd like to have, their favorite flavors of ice cream, what vegetables they like, and what brands of toothpaste they use. Quite literally, everything from soup to nuts is fair game for analysis by young mathematicians. Older children can take a poll, figuring out how much milk is consumed by their families. If a family consumes, say, 83 cups of milk a week, what size containers would that family need to buy? The problem might be complicated by the fact that not all family members drink the same type of milk; consumption of skim milk and two percent take the problem into health class.

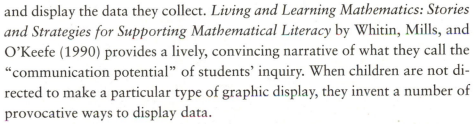

A large part of the fun, of course, is taking the survey. In classrooms where teachers feel the need for a neat and tidy display of mathematical thinking, they organize the children to vote on their favorite pet, for example. They make a large graph, and children post a picture they've drawn of their pet in the appropriate column: dog, cat, rabbit, or whatever. Older children may color in a square in the appropriate column—or hang a learning link as symbolic representation of their choice. The next step is to encourage the children to take some of the control, allowing for the mess and "inefficiency" of genuine student inquiry. Children choose their own survey questions and conduct the survey. They also figure out how best to organize and display the data they collect. *Living and Learning Mathematics: Stories and Strategies for Supporting Mathematical Literacy* by Whitin, Mills, and O'Keefe (1990) provides a lively, convincing narrative of what they call the "communication potential" of students' inquiry. When children are not directed to make a particular type of graphic display, they invent a number of provocative ways to display data.

SHOPTALK

Russell, Susan Jo and Rebecca Corwin. *Statistics: The Shape of Data.* Used Numbers: Real Data in the Classroom Series. Palo Alto, California: Dale Seymour Publications, 1990.

This book from the series Used Numbers: Real Data in the Classroom, helps teachers and children make a crucial point about data collection. "Students need to look at more than one representation of the data. Different students can see relationships in the data more clearly using particular kinds of representations, and different representations can illuminate different aspects of the data."

Students learn there are more ways to represent data than a bar graph. Becoming familiar with stem-and-leaf diagrams, number-line representations, and electronic spreadsheets allows different ways of seeing relationships.

When Marion Pelking's six year olds in Las Cruces, New Mexico, go apple picking, they survey classmates' responses to these questions:

- Do you like red apples or green apples?
- Do you like applesauce or apple pie?

Then they use real apples to make a graph on the one-foot-square floor tiles in their classroom.

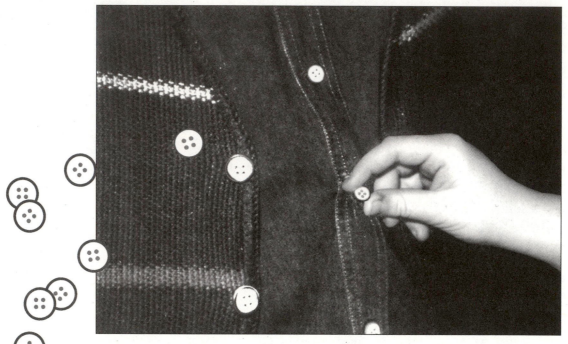

When Patricia Weaver asks her seven year olds in Tucson, Arizona, "How many buttons are we wearing today?" they make predictions: 99, 103, 51, 97, 91, 90, 110, 89, 88, and so on. Then the children begin to talk over how they might find out how many buttons are actually in the room. This class suggests that they

- put the children in line and count their buttons
- make a slash mark for every button each person is wearing and then add up the slash marks
- have Ms. Brooks (the Tucson math coordinator and frequent visitor to the classroom) figure it out.

The students' teacher affirms that "ask an adult" is definitely a logical choice; she also lets them know they need to make another choice, one where they aren't getting an adult to do their thinking.

As it turns out, Amy is the button queen; she is wearing 27 buttons; Sandie, Jane, and Julie aren't wearing any. The total number of buttons in this classroom is 90.

Once they have all this information, the children figure out a way to record their data so visitors can see what they've done. Thus, they are "inventing" graphs. Their teacher does not hand them a ready-made graph on which to stick their data.

In Fran Cohen's classroom in Cincinnati, Ohio, Peter, a six year old officially labeled learning disabled child, was so intrigued by graphs that he started collecting data. On his own, Peter kept track of what beverage each of his classmates chose for snack each day: milk, chocolate milk, or orange juice. He then devised his own system of graphing and reported the results to the class. The fact that Peter found his own problem is critical. Children who find problems in the real world are tapping into the power of mathematical inquiry.

Once children collect data and discuss their findings, they can extend their research. Children, for example, could discuss and chart things that scare them. A homework assignment might be for every student to ask two adults what scared them when they were young. Once children talk about their own fears, they may want to extend the project in directions that you hadn't envisioned. As Russell and Corwin reported in *Sorting: Groups and Graphs* from the series Used Numbers: Real Data in the Classroom (1990), some children want to find out what scares adults now rather than when they were young. This illustrates why it is important that children be given plenty of opportunity to talk about the results of their classroom research before extensions are made.

Finding the right question is often just as important a skill as finding the answer.

To help children understand mathematics in the real world, teachers are helping them to understand that finding the right question is often just as important a skill as finding the answer.

Through hands-on experience, children learn that the data we get depends on the questions we ask, that numbers don't exist separate from the decisions made by the number-gatherers. The key is encouraging children to be the questioners—as well as the answerers. This is a radical switch from asking them to fill in numbers in a workbook.

SHOPTALK

Ohanian, Susan. *Dates with the Greats: Being an Assembly of Anecdotes Embracing History, Literature, Science, Mathematics, Sports, Art, Music, and Popular Culture Collected for a Teacher's Pleasure and To Enrich and Enlighten the Lives of Children.* Chicago: Macmillan/McGraw-Hill, 1992.

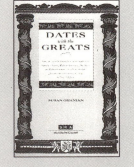

This book gives many ways to celebrate mathematics with students. It contains fascinating number stories relating to all subject areas.

Homework Hints

Homework for an eight year old might be interpreting a bar graph of the number of children in class who have birthdays each month. You might not ask any questions about this graph but, instead, ask children to report on what they learned from the graph, leaving it to them to ask their own questions after examining the data. Such a homework strategy helps both you and students learn that, in the real world, our questions don't come ready-made.

Classrooms that are engaged in this kind of work put an emphasis on inductive reasoning, encouraging students to engage in active mathematics. In these classrooms, children do math—they make observations, notice patterns, and form conclusions. This active mathematics is in contrast with a more deductive approach where students are trained to draw conclusions from given ideas that everybody accepts as true.

When we present mathematics to children as a "patternless" collection of manipulations and facts to be memorized, we cheat most of them of the opportunity to make their own discoveries and to encounter the deep underlying mathematical structures.

Graphing Fun Facts and Events

September
Celebrate Ice Cream. The ice cream cone was born at the St. Louis World Fair in 1904. Graph students' favorite ice cream flavor. Do ice cream preferences differ with grade levels? Do adults working in the school have different ice cream preferences?

October
Celebrate the Weather Bureau, created in 1890. Graph the weather for the month.

Celebrate Television, invented in the 1920s. Graph students' favorite TV shows.

Celebrate Halloween. Graph students' favorite Halloween costumes. In addition, they can graph the variety of loot received.

November
Celebrate Thanksgiving. Graph students' favorite Thanksgiving food.

Celebrate International Cat Week. Find the 10 most popular cat names in your school.

Celebrate Children's Book Week. Graph students' 10 favorite books. Maybe your students would like to find out what books teachers remember fondly from their childhood.

December
Celebrate Board Games. The Parker Brothers Company introduced *Monopoly* in 1936, and since then 250 million people have played the game. Who has played *Monopoly* in your class? What are the five most popular games in your class? in your school? Graph your findings.

January   *Celebrate Hobby Month.* Deltiology—what people who collect postcards do—is the third most popular collecting hobby. Can students guess what people like to collect even more? (stamps and coins) Graph what students like to do in their spare time.

Celebrate Oatmeal Month. Graph what students eat for breakfast.

Celebrate Pizza Week. What's the favorite pizza topping in your school?

February   *Celebrate Valentine's Day.* Graph the messages in Valentine's cards or on Valentine's candy. The New England Confectionery Company of Cambridge, Massachusetts, manufactures more than eight billion heart-shaped conversation candies each year, on sale only from January to Valentine's Day. The E. J. Brach company in Oakbrook Terrace, Illinois, makes around two billion hearts each year—enough, they say, to stretch from Loveland, Colorado, to Honey Pot Glen, Connecticut, 13 times.

Celebrate Sauerkraut and Frankfurter Week. Graph students' favorite thing to put on hot dogs.

Celebrate Potato Lovers' Month. Graph students' favorite way to eat potatoes.

March   *Celebrate Chocolate Week.* Graph students' favorite way to eat chocolate.

Celebrate Dr. Seuss's Birthday (1904). Find out the three favorite Seuss stories in your school.

April   *Celebrate Pets Are Wonderful Month.* Graph students' pets.

Celebrate Egg Salad Week. Graph students' favorite sandwiches.

Celebrate Earth Day. Graph students' ideas for celebrating Earth Day.

Celebrate the Opening of Baseball Season. Graph students' favorite teams and players.

May   *Celebrate Physical Fitness and Sports Month.* Graph students' favorite sports.

Celebrate Be Kind to Animals Week. Graph what animals students would like to be.

Celebrate Mother Goose Day. Graph the first Mother Goose rhyme teachers recite, when asked.

June   *Celebrate Zoo and Aquarium Month.* Graph students' favorite animals or fish.

Celebrate American Rivers Month. Graph the names of rivers students can name.

July   *Celebrate Beatrix Potter's Birthday* (1866). Graph the most popular Potter tales.

August   *Celebrate Anti-Boredom Month.* Graph students' advice for preventing boredom.

A Different View of Math

First it was a square...then eight year olds in Katy Rose's class at El Toro Marine School in Irvine, California, transformed it into a dog, a car, a television, a submarine, a bottle of glue, an alien, a kite, and a wedding. Then they published their ideas in a class book titled *First It Was a Square...*

By encouraging children to investigate spatial as well as numerical relationships, teachers hope to tap into what researcher on intelligence Howard Gardner calls spatial intelligence, one of the multiple intelligences that allowed such gifted individuals as Leonardo da Vinci to excel across a number of fields. The contribution of spatial intelligence is readily apparent, says Gardner, in such fields as sculpture or mathematical topology; it is also invaluable in providing a metaphor or model for scientific

process—witness the double helix pattern James Watson and Francis Crick used to describe DNA. Students who write books like *First It Was a Square...* are learning at a young age that mathematics includes mental images, transforming geometric constructs in your mind, and using your imagination to create new objects.

A 1990s update on the importance of spatial intelligence is posited by psychologists who study the condition of hostages released after long periods of captivity. Although conceding that many factors, including physical and psychological resources, are important to hostages' survival, psychologists are now taking a serious look at intellectual traits. Some hostages can construct new worlds in their minds; they invent new games, even new languages.

Psychiatrist Frank Ochberg of Michigan State University, talks of a hostage who "designed buildings in his head and planned exotic menus at various restaurants" (*Time*, August 26, 1991).

Make That the "Write" Answer

Students in Piedmont, California, write books about math. Inspired by Alvin Schwartz's *10 Copycats in a Boat,* Nancy Litton's combined class of first and second graders wrote the *Math Riddle Book.*

- What has 20 legs, 10 eyes, 5 heads, and 5 tails and sometimes lives in a barn?
  Answer: a pig with 4 piglets. *Elizabeth*
- What has four wings, twelve legs, and lives in the ground?
  Answer: two queen ants. *Nick*
- What has a nose on its head, a nose on its tail, and has four wings?
  Answer: a jet with one behind it. *Jeff*
- A soccer team won 6 to 0 but no boy made a goal. How come?
  Answer: because it was a girls' soccer team. *Taryn*
- If there was 1 copy cat in a boat and it turned over and there were 4,999 copy cats nearby how many would be in the water?
  Answer: 5,000. *Andrew*

Having students write about the mathematics they are working on has several benefits.

- Writing requires them to reflect on their understanding. When people of any age write, they think about what they know. In finding ways to put what they know into words, they explore and extend the boundaries of their understanding.

- Student writing helps you get inside your students' heads and find out both understandings and misunderstandings. When you focus on a student's process, you have a much clearer view of where the next lesson should go than you would if you were merely tabulating right and wrong answers.
- Asking students to write about their mathematics understanding sends an important message. You let your students know that their thinking is more important to you than a single, correct answer.

Classroom Strategies

As noted math educator Marilyn Burns points out in "Helping Your Students Make Sense Out of Math" (1988), "Writing has a place in math only if it stimulates the children to think and reason." Burns provides two strategies for getting your students to do just that.

1. When teaching number concepts, focus on problems that require written responses, not just numerical answers.

Park School eight year olds in Mill Valley, California, for example, were given the task of finding how many raisins were in their ½-ounce snack boxes. That done, they worked in groups of three to five to find out how many raisins they had altogether and how to share them equally. Their descriptions of the process show a range of mathematical understanding.

- We had 112 raisins. We passed out the raisins one at a time. We each got 37. We divided the one that was left into thirds.
- We had 175 raisins altogether. We counted them by fives, then divided them by five. We each got 35.
- We had 146 raisins. We divided 100 into four parts and we each got 25. After that, we divided the 40 into four parts. Then we each had 35. Then we divided the 6. We each ended up with 36½.

Although the methods of each group were different, they all worked. Most important, observes Burns, "they all made sense to the children." The teacher then used this sharing of raisins experience as a basis for the formal study of division. For more examples of child-centered methods of introducing math concepts to children see Marilyn Burns' series *Math By All Means: Multiplication Grade 3* (1991).

2. Use word problems that get students reasoning as well as finding answers.

Here's a popular problem that has travelled around the country: "A farmer had five cows and four chickens in a field. He wondered how many feet and tails there were altogether." Students solve this problem in pairs and are asked to record their solution, along with an explanation of how they solved the problem. Alamo School seven year olds in San Francisco, California, used different methods to find a solution.

- A cow has four legs and one tail, so that makes five each and that makes 25. A chicken has two legs and one tail so that makes 37.
- You get paper and you draw five cows and four chickens. You count the feet and tails. You add the tails and feet and you get your answer.

Students develop every-day skills when they learn mathematics through hands-on activities, writing, problem solving, and research.

Field Notes: Teacher-To-Teacher

Learning how and when to use a calculator is a vital skill. Calculators are always accessible in my classroom. Some children take calculators to their tables as soon as I announce "math time." And sometimes they discover that calculator answers can be confusing.

When I challenge students to figure out how 17 kings might share 42 elephants, Doug quickly punches the numbers into his calculator and comes up with 2.4705. "This makes no sense," he complains. I then talk about when calculator answers make sense and when they don't, stressing that calculators can work for you but they can't think for you.

Lynn Zolli
Jefferson School
San Francisco, California

DIALOGUE

What strategies do I use to engage students in thinking and reasoning? How do I assess their learning?

_____

_____

_____

_____

What new strategies would I like to try?

_____

_____

_____

_____

Chapter 2

Mathematics Across the Curriculum

We know that, as informed citizens, we are required to make mathematically informed decisions, not only about our jobs but about our government and our personal lives as well. Yet, how many people do you know who know what the national debt means? How many can figure out whether it's better to keep the home mortgage they have or to refinance? better to take the car loan offered by the dealer or to pay cash? On a simpler level, how many people do you know who groan after a restaurant meal when it's time to figure the tip? or feel stumped at the prospect of figuring out how much paint or wallpaper they need to redo a room?

When we make connections and expose students to math throughout the school day, we create a learning environment that prepares students for solving mathematical problems throughout their lives. Some points to remember:

- *There are many ways to find an answer to mathematical problems.* Students learn they can use a calculator, draw a picture, make a guess, or work backward. They can work with other students.
- *Mathematics is more than arithmetic.* Just as important as arithmetic are geometry, measurement, probability, statistics, patterns, functions, logic, and algebra.

```
┌──────────────────────────────────────────────────────────────┐
│                        D I A L O G U E                         │
│                                                                │
│  Name at least one way each group of people listed below use   │
│  math outside of the classroom.                                │
│                                                                │
│  Ages 4–8  _____ │
│                                                                │
│  Ages 9–12 _____ │
│                                                                │
│  Ages 13–16 _____ │
│                                                                │
│  Ages 17–21 _____ │
│                                                                │
│  Ages 22–35 _____ │
│                                                                │
│  Ages 36 and up _____ │
└──────────────────────────────────────────────────────────────┘
```

Students learn that math can inform their daily lives and arouse their social conscience.

From kindergarten on, children benefit from mathematical explorations that reveal the usefulness of mathematics in many subject areas. Children in Illinois construct tessellations (repeated geometric figures); six year olds in Albuquerque figure out how many children are present by knowing how many are absent. Seven year olds in Baton Rouge figure out how many vans they need for a field trip if seven children fit in one van and there are twenty-three children in the class. Eight year olds in San Francisco figure out how to divide their class of 28 into groups of 2, 3, 4, 5, 6, 7, 8, and 9. Nine year olds in Belgrade, Montana, make beautiful Fibonacci designs graphing number sequences—and teach their parents for homework. Ten year olds in Albuquerque incorporate Navajo art into their own original tessellation designs, while learning about Navajo culture.

Connecting to Social Studies

Data collection and display have a strong social studies focus. For example, kindergartners make pictographs of how they get to school: by bus, car, on foot, or by bike; upper grade youngsters examine the environmental implications of how their parents get to work.

Children collect and display data on things that scare them, favorite pets, favorite foods, and a multitude of other topics that interest them. Older students survey and study food eaten in the cafeteria; for example, they look at the nutritional content of what is eaten and what is thrown away. They learn that math can inform their daily lives—and arouse their social conscience.

DIALOGUE

Draw a sketch of what your math classroom looks like. Add a brief description of what children are doing.

Checklist

☐ Children are working with manipulatives, not just paper and pencil.

☐ Children are using calculators.

☐ Children are often working in small groups and talking with each other about their ideas and questions.

☐ Children are writing about mathematics—to clarify their own thinking and to explain it to others.

☐ Children are exploring mathematics in things that interest them in real life. Through this exploration they are developing number sense, working with measurement, geometry, and statistics.

Through math, students understand the increasingly complex world in which we live. This might start as collecting data about television commercials aimed at children, to creating and interpreting graphs on such social issues as handguns, segregated housing, and schooling. There are countless ways that math connects with social studies.

Time yourself. Ask students to keep a time diary for one week, writing down how much time they spend sleeping, eating, watching TV, attending school, playing outside school, and so on. They can express the results in hours, in a graph, as fractions, and so on.

Homework. Ask students to survey their school and neighborhood, looking for all the coin machines that sell things or dispense services—and their costs. They may come up with 30 cents for a telephone call, 25 cents for parking, 50 cents for cookies, 75 cents for laundry, or whatever. Encourage students to keep adding their new data to a running class list on a bulletin board.

After a week or so of discovering new machines, extend this homework with in-class problem solving. Younger students can figure out which coins they need to use for each machine. Challenge students to figure out how many coin combinations are possible if these machines required exact change.

U.S. flag math. The history of the U.S. flag contains interesting numerical display possibilities. Here are a few mathematical problems you could pose to students:

- Predict how you think the stars in the original 13-star flag were arranged.
- Figure out some good arrangements for our flag when it had 48 stars.
- Rearrange a 50-star flag.
- Predict what might happen if Puerto Rico or Washington, DC become states and you needed to arrange a 51-star or 52-star flag.

Some children immediately see the multiplication and division connection to the problems. Others need to draw pictures. Be sure to make manipulative materials available.

Supermarket Math

In "What's in a Receipt?" (*Learning 88*, January) Bob Tierney points out that grocery receipts can pave the way to critical thinking, science, math, and social studies. Tierney asks students to study a grocery receipt and guess who purchased the items. Was it someone shopping for a family? someone who lives alone? What's the age of the shopper? Does the person have pets? children? How can students tell? Tierney cautions students to be careful about distinguishing inferences from facts.

In "Supermarket Challenge" (*Arithmetic Teacher,* October 1992), Sharon Axelson also gives her students register tapes showing items bought during one visit to the grocery store. She asks students working in groups to classify the items, to organize their data into a table, and to display that data in a variety of graphs. Each team then writes five story problems based on their data. Finally, the teams write stories about a family who might have bought the items.

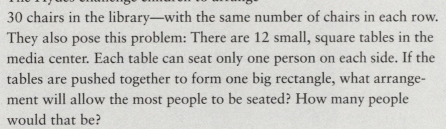

SHOPTALK

Hyde, Arthur A. and Pamela R. Hyde. *Mathwise: Teaching Mathematical Thinking and Problem Solving.* Portsmouth, New Hampshire: Heinemann, 1991.

Arthur and Pamela Hyde's book has interesting real-world variations on this problem: The Hydes challenge children to arrange 30 chairs in the library—with the same number of chairs in each row. They also pose this problem: There are 12 small, square tables in the media center. Each table can seat only one person on each side. If the tables are pushed together to form one big rectangle, what arrangement will allow the most people to be seated? How many people would that be?

The Hydes' book is filled with challenging problems that connect students' lives to mathematical concepts.

Math Trash

Students can use the mathematics of trash to examine problems that are caused by society and can be solved by a caring, knowledgeable citizenry. Ten year olds in Baton Rouge collected refuse for one week, keeping track of amounts and types. Then they figured out a way to report the results graphically. A classroom version of this is to keep track of the paper discarded in class every day for a week. Students should reflect on their data and make a plan for saving paper school-wide. Non-food and food refuse in the cafeteria are other possibilities for investigation.

Connecting to Language Arts

Language study becomes irresistible when students discover mathematical relationships. Ask students to write letters of the alphabet vertically on a piece of paper, then choose a page in a book and chart how many times each

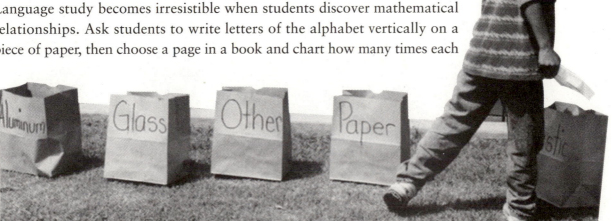

letter appears on that page. Students can reflect on what they have learned about language from statistical investigation, and express it in writing.

Students who speak a language other than English and who have access to printed material in that language might conduct the same investigation and see if the results are similar. Students can make a similar investigation on the length of words. How many one-letter words are on the page? How many two-letter words? three-letter words, and so on? They can do this in teams, with different team members keeping track of words of different lengths.

Ask students if they think all books would yield the same results. Record their predictions for, say, picture books, easy-read books, their science books, student magazines, and so on. Such a project can extend as far as student interest carries it. Engineering students at a technological university investigated word length and paragraph length (number of sentences in a paragraph) in everything from *TV Guide* to *Rolling Stone* to the university president's welcome address—with provocative results. Students were first startled, and then bemused, to discover that the only publication with shorter sentences than *TV Guide* was the university president's address.

Math can be integrated with language arts in countless ways. Some examples include having students read picture books that have powerful math themes, write their own riddle books and math problems, and keep math journals.

S H O P T A L K

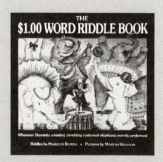

Burns, Marilyn. *The $1.00 Word Riddle Book*. White Plains, New York: Math Solutions/Cuisenaire Company, 1990.

This children's book provides an entertaining way for students to examine how words are put together. Burns asks: "If a = $0.01, b = $0.02, and so on, up to z = $0.26, then whose name is worth $1.00?" The book has over a hundred examples of $1.00 words, many presented as riddles. Students can make up challenging varieties: What's the least expensive synonym for a $1.00 word? Who has the most expensive name?

SHOPTALK

Krause, Marina. *Multicultural Mathematics Materials*. Reston, Virginia: National Council of Teachers of Mathematics, 1990.

This resource contains a number of projects ranging from ancient Egyptian games and tangrams to the Aztec calendar and the geometry of Hopi pottery.

Ohanian, Susan. "Record-Setting Math," *Learning 90,* May-June 1990.

This article shows how the *Guinness Book of World Records* (Sterling Publishing, annual) can spur students to find fascinating numbers in the world we live in.

National Council for the Social Studies. Theme Issue: "Social Mathematics Shapes Our View of the World," *Social Studies and the Young Learner,* September-October 1993.

Articles in this issue suggest activities that link social studies and mathematical content, processes, and purposes: data in democratic classrooms, timelines that mean something to children, the integration of global awareness and math.

Math Journals

Marsha Copenhaver's kindergartners in Orlando, Florida, and Lori Perlman's kindergartners in Skokie, Illinois, have something in common—they love their math journals. The children express their thoughts about their math work which their teachers record.

Beth Parker encourages her third graders in Albuquerque to explore their mathematical understanding through journal writing. She challenges them to push to the edge of their own understanding, letting them know that writing "I like fractions, they are fun" does not cut the mustard.

Parker responds to every student. The following exchange is typical:

Maria writes:

A fraction is something with numbers that is in times tables—I really don't know what a fraction is but I am trying hard so I still think a fraction is numbers. I have a question. Do all people learn fractions in fourth grade?

Dear Maria,

All children in New Mexico learn about fractions in fourth grade and fifth and sixth and…Maria, I am still learning about fractions!

Mrs. P.

Linda also expresses some disgruntlement with fractions:

A fraction is something with numbers like ½. It's a different way of doing math. Sometimes it isn't that fun but you learn some things that will help you later in your life. And sometimes I don't get stuff like when we were doing the work 'let 0 = 1 whole' and name 4 cubes but I'm learning it like today. I'm sort of getting the hang of it and sometimes I think it's fun but not all the time. It can be boring some of the time. Sometimes I don't get what you mean when it says on the board draw ⅓. Equivalent fractions are fun.

Dear Linda,

Thank you for letting me know how you are feeling about fractions and math class. Sometimes when you begin learning something new, like fractions, it is hard. What did you do with equivalent fractions that you enjoyed?

Mrs. P.

Field Notes: Teacher-To-Teacher

I tell my third-graders:

"We were doing something new today. I'd like you to respond in your math logs about what you learned. Tell me what you discovered by doing this. Tell me about what you need to think about and what you did. If you made a mistake, I'd like to hear about that, too. After all, mistakes are learning opportunities. They help you learn, and they help me, too."

Often when we've been working on something new, I ask the whole group to talk about it before they start writing in their journals. This gives children a mathematical vocabulary on which to draw. It stimulates their thinking and shows them that ideas are common currency in the room, that students should share ideas rather then hoard them.

Pam Hegler
Ernest Stapleton School
Rio Rancho, New Mexico

Reflections

Earlene Hemmer and Terri Goyins, primary grade teachers in Belgrade, Montana, suggest prompts for stimulating children's thinking and writing about the math activities in which they are engaged.

- What did you do today?
- What did you like or dislike about math today?
- How do you think we will use what we learned in class tomorrow?
- How will we use these materials?
- What really happened?
- What did you learn?
- What is _____? (Fill in the blank with the math concept under study.)

Literature

Children's literature can be a powerful stimulus to children's mathematical thinking—if they are encouraged to explore deep mathematical concepts and not just surface trivia. For example, sharing cookies is the theme of *The Doorbell Rang* by Pat Hutchins. Of course, children enjoy making their own cookies, but it is important to remember the mathematical focus is to encourage students to figure out how to share the cookies equally and thereby "invent" division.

When given the time and space to exercise their creative powers, children are even more fascinated by intellectual exploration than by stirring cookie dough. Here's how Lynn Zolli's student Adam constructed a system for dividing the cookies.

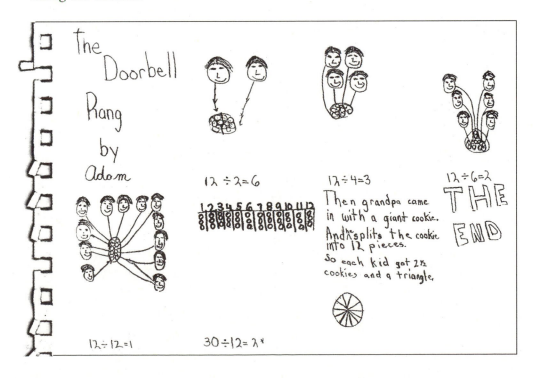

Moira's Birthday by Robert Munsch provides a less ordered mathematical universe for children to explore. It is, in fact, rather chaotic. Moira's parents tell her that for her birthday she can invite six kids, just one from each grade: "1-2-3-4-5-6; and NNNNNO kindergarten!"

So Moira invites six kids, but a friend who hadn't been invited begs to come, and Moira says "yes," and then another begs and another...by the end of the day, Moira has invited all of grade 1, grade 2, grade 3, grade 4, grade 5, grade 6, *aaaaand* kindergarten. But she doesn't tell her mother and father. She is afraid they might get upset.

How Moira figures out the food for her guests and then figures out what to do with all the presents makes for mathematical problem solving in a zany real-world setting. When first graders were asked how many birthday cakes Moira would need, Kevin said, "About a million." Melodie replied, "One. If it's big enough." John Holt reported in *How Children Fail* (1964) that when he asked a child, "Would you rather have ⅓ or ¼ of something to eat?" she said in a flash, "Depends what it is." These responses show how real problem solving involves interpretation and finding an answer—one of many—that makes sense.

See the Children's Bibliography for picture books that provoke exploration of powerful mathematics principles.

SHOPTALK

Burns, Marilyn. *Math and Literature (K-3).* White Plains, New York: Math Solutions/Cuisenaire Company, 1992.

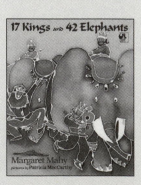

Math and Literature is especially helpful in providing classroom examples of picture books that spark children's exploration of deep mathematical principles. See, for example, Burns' samples of children's exploration of the concept of equal sharing (and their very clever resolution of the problem of remainders) when figuring out how 17 kings can share 42 elephants in Margaret Mahy's beautiful picture book *17 Kings and 42 Elephants,* illustrated by Patricia MacCarthy. Where traditional textbooks would seldom introduce division with a problem requiring remainders, third graders are not daunted by these leftovers.

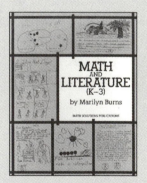

Finding Math Themes in Middle Grade Fiction

A line in *Tough-Luck Karen* by Johanna Hurwitz convinced Shirley Russell, who teaches a fourth-fifth grade combination class in Lincoln, California, to broaden her approach to mathematics. The heroine Karen has trouble with schoolwork, and she questions the relevance of that schoolwork. "In all her thirteen years, she had never seen her parents sit down and make a graph…" Karen challenges her teacher, "I bet you never made a single graph in your entire life." Russell felt challenged to make sure she showed her students the real-world relevance of graphs. For starters, she brought in plenty of graphs from newspapers. *USA Today,* for one, prints numerous graphs, often on topics of interest to children.

Russell set her students the task of finding other characters in their reading who have "attitudes" about math. They established a math quotation board. Here are some samples of what they found.

In *Erin McEwan, Your Days Are Numbered* by Alan Ritchie (Knopf, Bullseye, 1991)

> Math was a world of darkest confusion for Erin. She would rather be locked in a cupboard with a wild animal than forced to share her mind with a handful of numbers.

The Baby-Sitters Club: Claudia and the Middle School Mystery by Ann Martin (Scholastic, 1991)

> "So, if Gertrude used two thirds of a cup of chocolate to make eight cookies, how much chocolate would be in each cookie?" Janine asked.

> I frowned. I bit my lip. I tapped my pencil against my front teeth. "Each cookie would have. . ." Right then I hated Gertrude, whoever she was. Why did she have to make cookies, anyway? And why did she have to measure out the chocolate? I'd just dump in as much as I had. I love chocolate.

Your Move, J.P.! by Lois Lowry (Houghton Mifflin, 1990)

> He had been absorbed in a complicated problem about two cars—a Porsche and a Lamborghini—headed from Geneva to Monte Carlo in a race, and who would win by how many minutes if they each went so many kilometers per hour; but the Lamborghini got a late start by a few minutes and the Porsche had a mechanical problem along the way, which required two mechanics…

Minnie 'n Me: Gold-Star Homework by Lyn Calder (Disney Publishing Company, 1991)

> "If you have six friends and four ice cream cones, how many friends will not get ice cream?"

Russell's students were most scornful of the math homework they found in *Minnie 'n Me* published by Disney. Students complained "you wouldn't have to think about that," "it sounds just like the math books," "it doesn't sound real." They agreed with Jaime Escalante, noted math educator who, in a television special talked about the "fruit problem—all those apples and oranges we ask kids to add and subtract and pretend its problem solving."

Russell is impressed that children's literature has provided the source for on-going student observation of what math is really about. She notes, "Until we talked about the 'Disney problem,' I had not given my fourth and fifth graders credit for recognizing how phony most workbook-type math is. The Disney problem became an instant classic in our classroom. When students want to voice contempt for something, they call it 'just another ice cream problem.' The opposite is the Porsche problem. If contempt is saying 'just another ice cream problem,' admiration is 'there's a Porsche problem.'"

Students learn to think mathematically through exploration, through trial and error, through experimentation.

Positive Math Connections in Books

If math often gets a bad rap from much fiction for middle-graders, the *Mathnet Casebook* series by David Connell and Jim Thurman provides a lively antidote. Based on the *Mathnet* television program, this series of books features *Mathnet* detectives George Frankly and Pat Tuesday as they use their powers of reasoning to crack confounding cases—and jokes.

David Birch's *The King's Chessboard* teaches lessons about the wise and foolish, about grace and humility—and about awesome mathematical relationships. After reading this book, children can figure out their own doubling problems. What would a child's allowance be at the end of a month if she were paid one cent on the first day, two cents on the second day, four cents on the third day, and so on? How long would it take to have enough money to buy a bike —or a school?

SHOPTALK

Griffiths, Rachel and Margaret Clyne. *Books You Can Count On: Linking Mathematics and Literature*. Portsmouth, New Hampshire: Heinemann, 1991.

Whitin, David and Sandra Wilde. *Read Any Good Math Lately? Children's Books for Mathematical Learning, K-6*. Portsmouth, New Hampshire: Heinemann, 1992.

These books list numerous classroom-tested picture books that get children thinking about mathematics in creative, inventive ways. *Read Any Good Math Lately?* moves beyond the primary crowd, showing how literature ranging from Shel Silverstein's poems to a Charlotte Pomerantz picture book can help upper elementary students.

Connecting to Art

When it's time for math class, neither children nor adults usually think of art. Tessellations change their assumptions. Tessellations draw upon and combine the skills of mathematics and art. A tessellation is a repeated geometric figure, or pattern, that completely fills a plane—with no gaps. A good example of a tessellating pattern is the tile on a kitchen floor.

Examples of tessellations can be found in Islamic art and in the work of Leonardo da Vinci and M. C. Escher, among others. When students are asked to find tessellations in the world around them, they will notice brick walkways, wrapping paper and fabric, acoustical ceiling tile, and so on.

Field Notes: Teacher-To-Teacher

I wanted to do tessellations with my primary graders because I'd never done it before. Trying new things keeps me alive as a teacher.

Penny Vincent
Ernest Stapleton School
Rio Rancho, New Mexico

When children work to create their own tessellations, they are using their spatial sense, developing geometric awareness of how things fit in the real world, and satisfying an innate desire to create beautiful patterns. These patterns are what draw students to tessellations initially. The patterns are beautiful and challenging. Since manipulating polygons in space does not require numerical skill, this is a project that provides equal access to students of varying traditional mathematical talent; it gives all students opportunity to discover new skills and talents. It is as valuable for numerically adept students to discover that they have trouble with spatial configurations as it is for the not-so-good mathematicians to discover that they are especially adept at creating unique tessellating designs.

As students get more and more involved in the work, they see the usefulness of such geometric terms as polygon, rotate, and congruent. If they are exploring with pattern blocks, they will quickly learn the terminology of the blocks: square, triangle, hexagon, rhombus, parallelogram, and diamond.

You might introduce students to the idea of tessellating patterns through the use of pattern blocks or the "nibble technique." In this technique, students usually start with a 3 x 3 inch square. (Other polygons can be used, but the square is the easiest figure to start with.) They cut a "nibble" from one end, sliding that nibble to the opposite side and taping it. This becomes a template for covering a sheet of paper. Once students have covered their paper with this pattern, they look for ways to color their tessellated design. Here is a sample of a tessellation made by students in Louise Nielsen's fifth grade class in Rio Rancho, New Mexico.

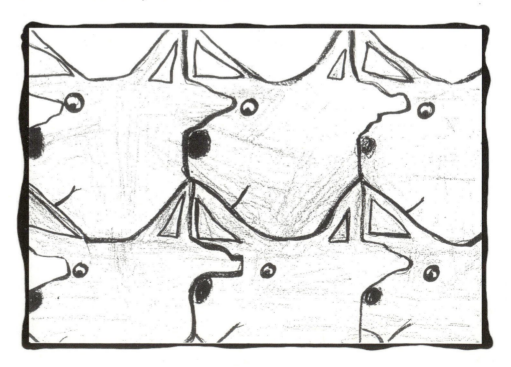

Park Ridge, Illinois, kindergarten teacher Lori Perlman uses pattern blocks to introduce her students to tessellations. "They are an immediate and total success," reports Perlman. "Children find tessellations irresistible. They are fascinated by the beautiful patterns they can create and will concentrate on this work for a very long time." Perlman says that in this work her five year olds reveal talents that they, their teacher, and their parents might not otherwise have discovered. Perlman laments that because of the short kindergarten day, tessellations are often considered to be an "extra," and squeezed into an already overcrowded schedule.

As a review of several months of pattern studies, Perlman asked her students to make any pattern they wanted. "When you're satisfied," she said, "you can tell me about your pattern. I'll take a picture of it, and we'll make a class pattern book."

Some students used beads or plastic animals to make A-B-A-B patterns, but the majority of children chose to use pattern blocks to construct intricate tessellations. When Perlman asked each child to describe his or her pattern, the tessellation-makers revealed the pleasure they take in showing off their knowledge of a new, sophisticated vocabulary.

Here's five-year-old Sam's pattern—and his comments:

> I made a star shape with pattern blocks. I started with a hexagon, then with triangles, then with diamonds, then with trapezoids, then with hexagons, then with squares, then with triangles. I thought the star shape was neat. It took a long time to make it.

Young Kasy reports both the problems of making tessellations on the floor—and a kindergartner's determination to make a beautiful pattern that will last.

> I made a tessellation on the floor with green triangles, blue diamonds, yellow octagon, no, not octagon, hexagon, only one, and what are these red things called? Yes, trapezoids, but somebody else stepped on it, so I wanted to do it on paper so they wouldn't ruin it. I made the tessellation with pattern block stickers. I liked doing it with the stickers because it's easier. It was neat. I want to learn and practice it, tessellations.

At times Perlman interrupts the construction of one child's pattern, asking other children what they think will come next. Here's Kasy's pattern at the point when Perlman interrupted, asking three other students to predict how many more blocks Kasy needed to finish his pattern.

SHOPTALK

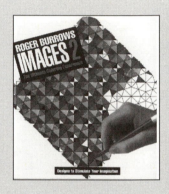

Burrows, Roger. *Images 2: The Ultimate Coloring Experience*. Philadelphia: Running Press, 1992.

Images 2: The Ultimate Coloring Experience helps students discover that coloring can be fun, rigorous, and satisfying. Students create their own patterns, which leads to heated discussions of symmetry. Students become symmetry detectives, trying to spot anomalies in each other's work. When a coloring project is underway, students of all ages keep their patterns in their desks, eagerly pulling them out whenever they have a spare moment. Middle graders glue back-to-back designs on poster board and then hang them in mobiles (creating balanced mobiles involves other mathematical skills). Even high schoolers in an alternative program for dropouts enjoy displaying their work. "I didn't know I had so much patience," revealed a 15-year-old frequent truant who worked on his pattern for eight days. He was so struck with its beauty, he shook his head, muttering, "I don't believe it." He posted it on the bulletin board and said, "I have an idea for another one."

For a look at symmetry in quilts see "Symmetry in American Folk Art" by Claudia Zaslavsky, in the Professional Bibliography, and *Eight Hands Round* by Ann Whitford Paul and *The Keeping Quilt* by Patricia Polacco, in the Children's Bibliography.

Going around in circles. Using a compass, students draw a circle design. Then they color the design so that no two sections next to each other are the same color. Challenge: What is the least number of colors one needs to do this?

How many triangles? Challenge students to count the triangles in this figure. Then challenge them to make a design puzzle for their classmates to solve. They could, for example, draw squares and ask how many squares are in their puzzle. Remind them they have to be the first to solve their own puzzle.

S H O P T A L K

National Council of Teachers of Mathematics. Focus Issue: "Spatial Sense." *Arithmetic Teacher*, February 1990.

This focus issue highlights spatial understandings necessary for interpreting, understanding, and appreciating our geometric world.

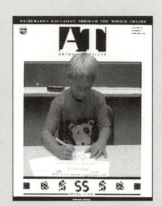

Dale Seymour. *Tessellation Winners: The First Contest*. Palo Alto, California: Dale Seymour Publications, 1991.

Featuring Escher-like original student work, this volume encourages students to explore geometric relationships and demonstrates how creative students can be.

Giganti, Paul, Jr. and Mary Jo Cittadino. "The Art of Tessellation." *Arithmetic Teacher*, March 1990.

You'll find ideas for getting students started with tessellations; includes the "nibble technique" of creating tessellating patterns.

Note: Tubs of pattern blocks are available from a number of companies such as Cuisenaire Company, Dale Seymour, and Delta Education.

Architecture Math

Architecture math is a way to help students find mathematics in the world around them. It requires no special materials—just the willingness to re-examine things we see every day. This mathematical awareness can then be expanded to broader cultures by inviting students to "walk through" library resources. Take students on a "geometry walk," asking them to find geometric shapes in the structures and environment they see such as buildings, playgrounds, and street signs.

Encourage students to browse through books picturing famous buildings—from the Taj Mahal to Monticello. Ask them to "find" shapes in these buildings. A variation on this activity is to compile a collection of pictures of famous buildings. Mount these pictures on cards and laminate them so they will stand wear and tear. Invite children to "choose a building" and research it. They should be prepared to tell their classmates three facts, including at least one mathematical fact, about the building.

Invite students to rearrange the classroom—mathematically. Using graph paper, they should make a scale drawing of the room. Remind them to include such built-in items as closets, doors, and windows. Then tell them to measure and cut out pieces of paper for the furniture. They can use glue to affix these items to their room plans. Working in teams, students can come up with suggestions for room rearrangement. Each team proposes a design for change and the class votes on which one to implement.

Connecting to Science

Children's bodies provide an irresistible mathematical link to science. Ask them to think of things they can measure—everything from a foot to their widest smile. They should record their estimate for each of these body parts and then record the accurate measurement. Have each child record his or her height and reach. Graph the results.

Ask students how far they think the class would extend if everyone were to lie down head to foot.

You can also challenge students to count parts of their body. This chart can get them started.

Find out your body numbers			
1	head… and what else?	24	ribs
2	eyes… and what else?	70	?
4	?	206	bones
10	?	5 mil	?

Students can be encouraged to add their own number facts to a body chart in the room.

Looking at your foot. Each student traces his or her foot on centimeter square paper. After figuring the area of the foot in square centimeters, each student cuts a piece of string equal to the perimeter, then tries to find people and objects with the same perimeter. Students can write down their estimates first.

SHOPTALK

Ohanian, Susan. "How To Measure a Pig and Other Math Secrets," *Learning 86*, October 1986.

This article tells stories of children who are encouraged to think about their world—and to think and write about what they discover.

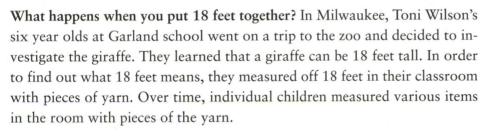

Eichelberger, Barbara and Connie Larson. *Constructions for Children: Projects in Design Technology*. Palo Alto, California: Dale Seymour Publications, 1993.

This resource features real-world problem-solving activities using everyday materials and creativity. Inventions are grouped into different design systems, including gravity power, gears, levers, and structures.

What happens when you put 18 feet together? In Milwaukee, Toni Wilson's six year olds at Garland school went on a trip to the zoo and decided to investigate the giraffe. They learned that a giraffe can be 18 feet tall. In order to find out what 18 feet means, they measured off 18 feet in their classroom with pieces of yarn. Over time, individual children measured various items in the room with pieces of the yarn.

"See if you can find something that's about this long," Toni Wilson invited them to explore again and again. Children discovered that the chalkboard and the bulletin board are nearly the same length, 18 feet. In their reading they discovered that *Tyrannosaurus rex* was about 18 feet in height. They came back to the height of the giraffe again and again. They found out how many people it took to make 18 feet; they speculated on how many fourth graders it might take, how many adults.

In Rio Rancho, Pam Hegler read *How Big Is a Foot?* by Rolf Myller to her primary graders as a way of introducing the importance of standard measure. This is a comical story about the troubles a king gets into when he wants to give the queen a bed for her birthday. Beds haven't been invented yet, and so the king has the queen lie on the floor, wearing her crown which she sometimes likes to wear to sleep; and he paces off her length—six feet. Problems arise because the carpenter's feet aren't nearly so long as the king's.

Worm and other creature math. Molly McLaughlin's *Earthworms, Dirt, and Rotten Leaves* inspires students to look closely at worms. By extension, it also provides a model on how to look closely at other creatures. Here is a sample from the "Earthworm Observation Guide":

1. What shape is the earthworm?
2. How long is it? How did you measure it?

3. How does the worm move?

4. How fast does it go?

5. What happens when the worm meets another worm?

6. Surprises (Leave some space to write down observations you didn't think of beforehand, and questions you think of to ask.)

The question "How did you measure it?" provides stimulating possibilities for all sorts of scientific investigation.

- How do environmental scientists measure, for example, a bear's age?
- How do astronomers measure the distance to other planets and the stars?
- How do geologists measure the temperature of the earth?
- How do doctors measure blood pressure, and what do those numbers mean?

How would students find out the answers? What other questions about measurement do they have? What would they like to measure, and how would they go about it?

Measuring the world. Ask students to record the temperature every hour they are in school for one week. After they make a graph of their findings, they can write and talk about what their graphs show. Challenge: How might students set up a measurement experiment that would show that the sun's relationship to the earth changes over time?

S H O P T A L K

Garland, Trudi Hammel. *Fascinating Fibonaccis: Mystery and Magic in Numbers.* Palo Alto, California: Dale Seymour Publications, 1987.
This book discusses Fibonacci relationships in science and technology as well as in art, poetry, and the stock market.

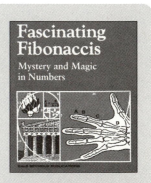

Baker, Ann and Johnny Baker. *Raps and Rhymes in Maths.* Portsmouth, New Hampshire: Heinemann, 1991.
Ann and Johnny Baker's *Raps and Rhymes in Maths* builds on children's enjoyment of rhythmic chanting and clapping to a beat. This collection of traditional and modern rhymes, riddles, and stories with mathematical themes provides challenge as well as entertainment.

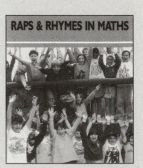

Chapter 3

Manipulatives—Tools for Learning

Across the country, teachers working to change the way they present mathematics to their students look to manipulative materials. Manipulatives give students hands-on experiences with the abstractions of mathematical principles. From Conecuh County, Alabama, to Albuquerque, New Mexico, primary grade teachers stock their classrooms with connecting cubes, pattern blocks, sets of tangram puzzles, geoboards, linking materials, and Cuisenaire rods.

Although suddenly they're the hot new thing in education, manipulative materials are not really new. Connecting cubes, for example, were first introduced in 1953. In *How Children Fail,* a book as mindful and helpful today as when it was first published in 1964, child psychologist and teacher's teacher John Holt observed, "The beauty of the Cuisenaire rods is not only that they enable children to discover, themselves, how to carry out certain operations, but also that they enable them to see that these operations really work, really describe what happens."

Despite plenty of research documenting the value of providing concrete ways to help students understand mathematical concepts, manipulatives have had a hard time catching on. There is optimism that a clarion call for manipulative materials in the NCTM Standards will put manipulatives into the hands of students—at all grade levels.

```
╔══════════════════════════════════════════════════╗
║                   D I A L O G U E                  ║
║                                                    ║
║   Think of a change in the content of mathematics  ║
║   curriculum since you were in elementary school.  ║
║   Is there something my students want to know      ║
║   that I didn't know as recently as five years     ║
║   ago? What is it?                                 ║
║   _____   ║
║                                                    ║
║   _____   ║
║                                                    ║
║   What experiences have I had that revealed the    ║
║   beauty and power of mathematics?                 ║
║   _____   ║
║                                                    ║
║   _____   ║
║                                                    ║
║   How could I help my students to see some beauty  ║
║   and power in mathematics study?                  ║
║   _____   ║
║                                                    ║
║   _____   ║
╚══════════════════════════════════════════════════╝
```

Seven-year-old students in Pam Spencer's classroom at the Field School in Columbia, Missouri, rotate among activity stations featuring manipulatives, including:

- connecting cubes—measurement
- pattern blocks—multiplication
- inset pattern boards—patterns
- learning links—multiplication
- fraction pieces—fractions
- base ten blocks—subtraction

Spencer has in no way abandoned skills. Students are spending much less time on paper-and-pencil skill drill. They are gaining experience with several skills at the same time. They don't have to "master" subtraction facts before they move to fractions or multiplication. They experience the same skill through a variety of approaches. With manipulative materials they work on multiplication, for example, both from a numerical and a geometric perspective.

Spencer does not tell her students that the pattern blocks and the learning links are both dealing with multiplication; she does not tell them that a geometric approach to multiplication gets at the same relationships as a numerical approach. Young Jeanne is excited to discover this on her own. "Hey! I was multiplying over there, and now I'm doing it here! It's different but it's kind of the same." The child who makes this intuitive leap knows firsthand the power and the beauty of mathematics. It is a power and beauty not available from workbook exercises.

The focus of instruction has shifted to teaching for an understanding of fundamental concepts. To this end, teachers design instructional experiences so that children are exposed to several goals at the same time. Knowing the facts are still important, but they are not sufficient. Students are expected to know when to use the facts; they are expected to be flexible, to be able to adapt what they know to new situations.

S H O P T A L K

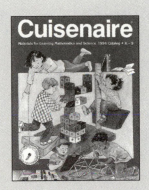

Cuisenaire Company of America, *Learning With…Teacher Guides*. White Plains, New York: Cuisenaire Company, 1992-95.

What manipulatives will you want to have in your classroom? Cuisenaire offers a way for teachers to get started with manipulative materials by providing a free teacher's guide with the purchase of a set of manipulatives. Many guides are also available in Spanish. One set is inexpensive and usually enough for three or four students to work on together. Pattern blocks and base ten blocks do not come in small quantities however. Without hesitation, I advise that no classroom should be without pattern blocks. They bring beauty and order to the world.

Learning With…Teacher Guides are available for linking materials, two color counters, pattern blocks, base ten blocks, snap cubes, geometric fraction shapes, tangrams, attribute shapes, Cuisenaire rods, color tiles, fraction squares, geometric solids, and geoboards.

It's important to realize that you don't use one type of manipulative for one skill and another type for another skill. A Cuisenaire teacher's guide on linking materials gives advice that is generic to most manipulatives. Pointing out that these brightly colored 1 x 1 inch plastic links can be used for everything from counting and comparison to graphing and geometry, the guide stresses the importance of free exploration. Once students have explored on their own, teachers might want to ask them to figure out how many links they would have to put together to reach across their desks. Once they have determined this, they can predict—and verify—how many links would be needed to measure other objects in the room. Other activities are suggested. Significantly, these activities are not grade specific but are suitable across many grades. The key sentence in the guide is this: "After students have experimented with links, ask them to talk about what they discovered." Such advice applies, of course, not just to links but to all manipulatives. Ask the children.

Connecting cubes. Both Unifix and snap cubes are ¾ inch connecting cubes and come in 10 colors. Snap cubes connect on all sides. Multilink cubes also come in 10 different colors and are metric in size—two cm on each edge.

Cubes are useful in helping students learn a wide range of number concepts; they can be counted one-by-one or joined together to form lengths of any number.

Recommended amounts: a set of 100 cubes for four to six students.

Pattern blocks. Available in wood or plastic, the blocks come in six geometric shapes and colors and are easily the most popular manipulative material. Students use them to explore patterns, geometry, area, symmetry. Even more important, students use them to create the beauty of patterns. It is intuitive and necessary; you see these blocks and you have to make a pattern.

Recommended amounts: You can never have too many. A class of 25 students needs a minimum of five buckets.

Attribute materials. Attribute materials, whether they are attribute blocks or attribute links, contain the standard attributes of color, size, shape, and thickness. Students count, classify, sort, and create order; they investigate shape, size, area, and functional relationships. Most sets contain five shapes, three or four colors, two thicknesses, and two sizes.

Recommended amounts: One set for four students.

Color tiles. Color tiles are square 1 x 1 inch tiles that come in a set of four colors. Each set contains 400 tiles, 100 of each color. Tiles are used for counting, graphing, patterning, logic, probability, area and perimeter, multiplication, and fractions.

Recommended amounts: One set for 10 to 20 students.

Cuisenaire rods. Available in plastic or wood, the rods are sized from one unit to 10, each size being a different color. The association of size and color encourages younger children to investigate addition and subtraction and to make visual confirmation of these concepts. Older students use rods to investigate multiplication and division, as well as symmetry and spatial problem solving, area, perimeter, and volume.

Recommended amounts: One set of 155 rods for three to five students.

Base ten blocks. These materials extend the rods to three-dimensional squares and cubes. They are used to provide a physical model of place value, helping children to learn to "regroup."

Recommended amounts: Available in starter sets for four to six students or intermediate sets for 20-25 students.

Geoboards. Square boards with pegs come in different sizes and are made of different materials. The most common size has five rows of five pegs each. Some have a circular lattice of pegs on the alternate side of the board. Boards are used to investigate geometric shapes, symmetry, angles, perimeter and area, and fractions.

Recommended amounts: One board for each student.

Field Notes: Teacher-To-Teacher

You cannot make children responsible for what they have not been taught to do. You can't say "Don't leave the place a mess!" if you haven't taught them to be neat. When I introduce a manipulative, I role-play with a student putting that manipulative in its place. When I perceive a problem in management of materials, I interrupt the lesson and we role-play again. We role-play what we value—how to keep ourselves and our classroom organized as well as how to cooperate and help each other.

Patricia Jiminez Weaver
Drachman Primary Magnet School
Tucson, Arizona

The Value of Order

Teachers who are veteran advocates of the value of manipulatives agree that setting up a management system is essential to provide an effective learning environment and to maintain manipulative materials. In San Francisco, Lynn Zolli explains, "In the beginning of the year, I explain that this isn't my classroom; it is ours. I emphasize that we have to work together to keep things orderly." Zolli does not have 30 students rushing around the room putting things away. Throughout the day she asks for a single volunteer. "Who will help me by collecting all the scissors? Who will collect the glue?" And so on. Before the class lines up for recess, she suggests, "If everybody will pick up three pieces of paper before we go to line, we'll leave a clean room. I know you might not have dropped the paper, but we all need to help clean up." Zolli emphasizes that all classroom supplies must have a regular place. Pattern blocks have a bin that is always in the same place on the shelf. Calculators are stowed in the same place all year. All these materials are readily accessible to students.

Barbara Denu, primary grade teacher at Goodwood Elementary School in Baton Rouge, Louisiana, makes one person at each four-person table responsible for getting and returning supplies for one week at a time. That is the only person who goes to the manipulative baskets. "I find that the children usually organize the material much better than I do!" reports Denu.

Denu feels that another important part of the children's care of materials is the feeling of ownership. "We use what's available," says Denu. "Many of the manipulative materials in our classroom come from the children's homes and from their explorations: cotton balls, beans, toothpicks, acorns, pinecones, popcorn, cereal, and so on. Children feel protective of materials that they have helped supply."

SHOPTALK

Markle, Sandra. *Math Mini-Mysteries*. New York: Atheneum, 1993.

In this children's book, youngsters will learn how they can use math for everything from checking if the wind is right for kite-flying to measuring acid rain. They'll learn how math made it possible to carve the faces of four presidents on Mount Rushmore.

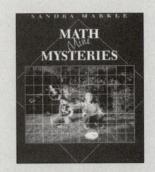

Children need to do what "real" mathematicians do— explore and invent for the rest of their lives.

Discoveries and Inventions

Sally Walker, primary teacher in Las Cruces, New Mexico, is as excited as her student Andrew when he invents a pattern during "free exploration" with his geoboard. This point is significant: Free exploration is not a concept that is satisfied during the first 15 minutes the children are exposed to manipulatives and then never returned to again. Children need to do what "real" mathematicians do—explore and invent for the rest of their lives. And so, late in the school year, Walker's students are still freely exploring. Andrew brings Walker a pattern: 5 rubber bands placed horizontally and 5 rubber bands placed vertically. Andrew says, "I've made 4 squares and 4 squares. That makes 8. And there are 8 and 8—that makes ___." He pauses and then continues, "7 and 7 are 14, so 8 and 8 are 16." Andrew is pleased, and so is his teacher. This sixteen-year veteran teacher says she is reinvigorated by her understanding of math teaching. "I have a doubles chart on the back wall," she says, "but isn't it ever so much better that Andrew discovered this on his own?" Walker adds, "I enjoy teaching math more than ever before and I would never go back to teaching math from a traditional textbook. Seeing the children discover their own math makes me proud to be a teacher."

Concrete, hands-on materials don't have to come in a kit. Barbara Denu's students in Baton Rouge bring in cotton balls and popcorn. Glenda Stone, primary teacher at the W. O. Palmer Elementary School in Greenville, Alabama, brings in two large sacks full of loose socks. "My husband's socks need to be sorted into pairs," she says. "Can you estimate how many pairs there might be?" School has only been in session a bit over a week, so children have not had much opportunity to hone their number sense. Estimates range from 10 pairs to 1,000, and all the estimates are put on the board. Children sit in two large circles and, working in groups of two, sort the socks into pairs. One child worries that he doesn't want to touch somebody else's dirty socks. "No, honey, they're clean," his teacher assures him. When all the socks are sorted into pairs, Stone asks, "Who can tell me how we can find out how many pairs of socks we have?" She reminds the children that each child has two pairs of socks. After some discussion, the children decide to count by twos. There are 42 pairs. Since one child guessed 43, everyone expresses great amazement at how close she was.

Stone points to lots of guesses that are close to show that a guess doesn't have to be "right" to be good. She tells her students, "I've been teaching 25 years, and this is the first time I've brought socks to school. I just got up this morning and told my husband, 'I need all your socks—and I need them to be separated.' Can you imagine? I used to teach math from a book."

Stone points out that just having manipulative materials available brings change. "You can't do things the same way when you have different materials to work with." Last year, when Stone's group counted to 1,000 for the first time, her husband, vice president at a local bank, brought in a $1,000 bill for them to touch and even hold. Quite some manipulative!

Stone confesses, "I was nervous about this move to different materials. For twenty years I worked in a structure provided by the textbook. And now I feel compelled to learn a new structure. One thing, using manipulative materials cuts down on paperwork. There's no paperwork connected with sorting socks," Stone laughs. "But don't get me wrong. I haven't made this change because of the paperwork. I do it because it makes sense for children."

D I A L O G U E

What manipulatives do I use outside of the classroom?

_____

_____

A Caution on Manipulatives

When children in school are answer-centered rather than problem-centered, they don't see school as a place to learn but as a place where they must get the work done. In *The Informed Vision* (1974), professor and astute observer of children's thinking David Hawkins points out that when teachers try to streamline the use of manipulatives—and prevent their deviant use—instead of "managing materials," teachers are actually misusing those materials.

For example, one district mandates the use of manipulatives. The math curriculum supervisor sends out stacks of grade-level lessons for using manipulatives. Here's a sample activity sheet for one lesson. Each student is expected to fill in the blanks in this worksheet.

My pencil is _____ links long.

My book is _____ links long.

My shoe is _____ links long.

By over-organizing the child's experience with links, the worksheet takes all initiative from the child.

Hawkins laments that too often teachers focus on what concept children *should* get out of exposure to a particular concrete object rather than concentrating on what children actually get out of working with that material. Hawkins insists that when young children make a "cross-connection," when they jump from math to science to art, when an examination of hexagons leads to crochet patterns, when Fibonacci numbers lead to rabbits or tree growth, we should celebrate, not insist that the children immediately get back "on task."

A more free-form lesson might invite children to

- figure out what they are going to measure
- figure out what information to record—and in what form.

This exploration could lead to graphs of the shortest and longest items in the room or to a school-wide exploration, as took place in School 12 in Troy,

New York, to find out who wore the biggest shoe in the school. The excitement and exhilaration of asking the principal if you can measure his shoe is diluted if it is the teacher's assignment and not the child's idea. At School 12, children's shoe outlines were displayed in the hallway next to an outline the size of Michael Jordan's shoe—as well as the principal's.

Just as children learn to read by reading, so, too, do they learn mathematics by doing mathematics.

When a district mandates goals and materials, when it links manipulatives so closely with specific skills and tells teachers, "You use linking materials for this and connecting cubes for that," district policy makers are treating manipulatives like textbooks and thereby guaranteeing, at best, that children will not get anywhere near maximum benefit from the manipulatives. At worst, these policy makers are mandating failure for manipulatives.

This is a very difficult issue, and we are talking about hardworking, well-meaning people of good intent struggling with difficult questions. The tough issue is coming to grips with what you believe about how children learn. Once you do this, you are better equipped to make decisions about how to use manipulatives.

Certainly it isn't good enough to speak in high moral terms of getting rid of the workbooks and bringing in brightly colored tubs of manipulatives. If we use these manipulatives in pretty much the same ways we used workbooks—as busy work to keep children reasonably quiet while we are occupied "doing" reading groups—then we shortchange the manipulatives and the children, too.

Just as children learn to read by reading, so, too, do they learn mathematics by doing mathematics. They need a lot of uninterrupted time to explore, to experiment with materials and ideas. If they are using manipulatives, they need plenty of time to experiment, to engage in "off-task" speculation. If a child is engaged and involved in mathematical investigation, the child may need to work several days—or weeks—on the same problem. Sometimes you will decide when it's time to move on; sometimes the child will need to persevere.

Professor David Hawkins agrees and advises that neither child nor teacher make *all* the decisions. There is room for negotiation.

Derrick was a student in such a classroom at School 12, in Troy, New York, where I taught a multiage group of children. The children chose from a variety of math-science centers, knowing that once a choice is made they could have all the exploration time they needed—but, once chosen, they could not quit a center until they had worked through certain required problems. Derrick, a child of distressed family circumstances, chose the weighing station and over the period of a week weighed just about everything that was not nailed down. He often started each day by weighing my lunch. It became a class joke. Derrick would announce the weight in grandiose tones, "And today, Mrs. O's lunch weighs…," and everybody would laugh. Then, in one of those moments teachers wait for their whole career, Derrick decided to weigh bottle caps. Over the period of three hours, Derrick made the discovery that 30 bottle caps on one side of the balance weighed the same as 30 bottle caps on the other. This was not a problem I had set for Derrick; he came up with it on his own. About half an hour into his experiment, I realized something important was happening and started videotaping. Since I often turned the camera on and left it running while the class and I went on about our work, the children were used to the camera and nobody paid any attention to it.

Field Notes: Teacher-To-Teacher

I learn a lot from watching my videotapes. Once, an unplanned benefit ensued. Tapes of the children's explorations proved invaluable in convincing a working class neighborhood that changing the curriculum radically was a good idea. Parents came to view tapes; they came back bringing their neighbors to see. The tapes were the subject of several PTA programs, where parents asked if they could use the manipulative materials and try some of the projects they saw on tape.

—SO

During the three hours Derrick worked at this problem, the room was busy with the activities of 30 other children. Derrick would go "off task." Someone would show him a dinosaur mobile or the contents of a color chemistry test tube. He'd be distracted for a few minutes and then get on with his weighing. When he was close to discovery, he'd try to trick the balance, throwing an extra on quickly or stealing one away with a very careful, light touch. Finally, he was convinced and, since my hard and fast rule was write up your experiment, he wrote:

30 bottle caps = 30 bottle caps

The next morning, Derrick rushed into the room and started weighing bottle caps. He quickly confirmed that what was true the day before was still true: 30 = 30. Then he confirmed that 22 = 22. He muttered, "I wish I had 1,000 bottle caps." Then he weighed 1 inch cubes, confirming that 30 = 30. Derrick taught me something we teachers often take for granted—that once children learn a math fact, they haven't necessarily learned it forever. When we learn something today, we need to learn it tomorrow, too. More than that, he taught me that children need to be convinced that not only are numbers consistent and reliable, so are physical objects. Those bottle caps are the same density today as they were yesterday. Some of us need more reassurance about this stability than do others.

Derrick was getting answers by himself. These answers made sense to him. He was in charge both of the materials and of the questions being asked about those materials. Some people insist that this boy was "behind" his grade level, that he needed to spend his time drilling math facts so that he could catch up to his peers. But children who drill and drill on number facts that make no sense to them are worse off in the end than when they started. Not only do they fail to make sense of numbers, they end up fearing them. If Derrick explores enough with manipulative materials, if he moves on from those bottle caps to rods and cubes, he will get to the point where he can manipulate numbers in his head. When he gets to that point, it will be time to introduce conventional symbolism—using numbers as symbols.

I should note that while Derrick was weighing various materials, there was a whole lot of fun when all the cubes came tumbling down. A teacher has to put up with a lot of mess and noise during genuine discovery and learn to ignore it. Years later I participated in a university study on ambiguity. After administering their personality test, the good professors announced I had a tremendous tolerance for ambiguity. I told them it was no surprise; I'd cut my teacherly teeth on learning centers.

Again, John Holt's *How Children Fail* is worth quoting:

We make a serious mistake in asking children to perform symbolically operations which they could not perform concretely. A child should be able to find out which [group of Cuisenaire rods] has the most whites, a group of 37 or a group of 28, and how many more it has, before he is asked to do a problem like 37–28. And he should be able to do this latter kind of problem easily before [being] given a rule for doing it. So with all the operations of arithmetic. Numerical arithmetic should look to children like a simpler and faster way of doing things that they know how to do already, not a set of mysterious recipes for getting right answers to meaningless questions.

Children don't learn from other peoples' cookbook recipes, whether those recipes come with manipulative materials or in workbook pages. It matters little that we teachers know the best way to use those materials; what matters is that children be given the room to use and learn from those in the way that best fits their individual structures of knowledge.

SHOPTALK

Burns, Marilyn. *Mathematics: With Manipulatives.* (6 videos and teacher discussion guides). White Plains, New York: Cuisenaire Company, 1992.

Some districts make available to their teachers Marilyn Burns' series of six twenty-minute videotapes. On each of five tapes, Burns demonstrates the use of a particular manipulative, including base ten blocks, color tiles, Cuisenaire rods, geoboards, and pattern blocks. On the sixth tape she offers six models: Unifix cubes, Multilink cubes, color cubes, attribute blocks, tangrams, and two-color counters. What is especially striking to the neophyte user of manipulatives is the unified field revealed from watching all six tapes. We see the same mathematical concept being approached from a different angle using a different manipulative. This illustrates not so much whether the teacher is working with pattern blocks or geoboards, but the children's understanding of a concept and how that understanding can be enhanced through exploration with manipulatives. We see what really matters is that the teacher has a belief system firmly in place, one that extends far beyond the use of manipulatives. Burns raises issues of praise, autonomy, telling students when they're wrong, and a host of other concerns vital to teachers and she challenges the viewers to think about how to answer them.

E. D. Hirsch, an English professor who popularized the notion of cultural literacy, wrote a series of books called *What Your First Grader Needs To Know, What Your Second Grader Needs To Know* (1991), and so on, published by Doubleday. Hirsch echoes a concern of parents and teachers when he urges that second graders memorize the times tables. Hirsch insists that second graders should practice reciting "Six times two equals twelve. Seven times two equals fourteen."

In Hirsch's words, "With much (and regular) practice, students will be well prepared for mathematics in the third grade, and beyond." Mathematics experts disagree. In his celebrated book *On the Shoulders of Giants: New Approaches to Numeracy* (1990), Lynn Arthur Steen says that a skill-memorization focus is a "layer cake approach to mathematics education." It means that students never see the present-day relevance of mathematics but are always memorizing something as a way to "get ready" for the memorization that is to come in the next grade. Instead, insists Steen, we need to build curriculum with greater vertical continuity; we need "to connect the roots of mathematics to the branches of mathematics in the educational experience of children." Steen advocates "multiple parallel strands, each grounded in appropriate childhood experience."

We need to help children see the patterns of numbers rather than requiring students to memorize before they understand.

This means that we need to help children see the patterns of numbers rather than requiring students to memorize before they understand. Rather than presenting mathematics as separate, sequential skill chunks, such as the multiplication table, we expose children to the function of multiplication, encouraging them to "invent" and create multiplication strategies. Thus, six year olds may work on problems requiring multiplication or division while they are still learning to add. It means that students don't wait until age 15 for geometry but start learning it in kindergarten.

Teaching a demonstration lesson for teachers in the Exxon Education Foundation K-3 Math Project, Baton Rouge teacher Norah Miller showed what children can do when they are encouraged to solve real problems. She presented her primary graders with this problem:

> Our bus has broken down so we need to get back to school in a different way. The people here at the hotel have offered to drive us back in their hotel vans. We can fit seven children in each van so I need you to figure out how many vans we will need to get back to school.

Miller deliberately left out a piece of important information. After all, real-world problems don't come in neat and tidy packages. Real-world problem solvers have to figure out what information they need. Miller's students quickly figured out what information was missing—how many children and adults needed rides—they decided there were 20 students and two adults in their group.

Working in teams of two, students approached the problem in a variety of ways:

- Some students drew vans with seven passengers in each one.
- Some students built vans out of cubes.
- Some students used tally marks.
- Some students used repeated addition, adding 7 + 7 + 7 + 7 until their sum went over 22.

Emphasizing that answers aren't valuable without explanations, Miller asked each group to explain and justify their answer.

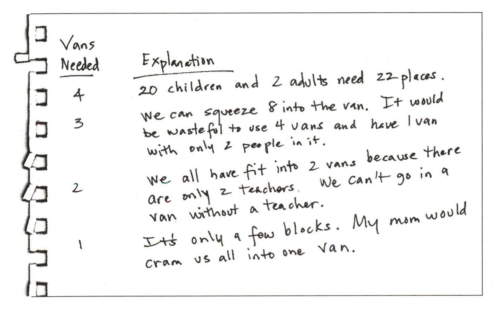

Miller explains that she is always looking for opportunities to invite students to solve real-life problems. She encourages her students to notice problems that require mathematical thinking. In her words, "It gets really exciting when the students think of problems that we need to solve." For this to happen, Miller knows that she must create a classroom where

- students are encouraged to use mathematics to figure out their real world
- students learn to work with others to solve problems
- students develop a language of mathematics—a way to think and talk mathematically.

Rather than presenting her students with a "layer cake curriculum" where they are memorizing facts to get ready for the next grade, Miller looks for ways to help children see real-life math connections ranging from the practical to the poetic.

In Temecula Valley, California, Blanche Raye shares this vision of mathematics with her students at Vail School. Her kindergartners are doing their math in the parking lot. "Education shouldn't be confined to one room," she comments. And so her students are estimating how many cars are in the parking lot. "Remember," she tells students, "estimation means 'take a good guess.'"

Along with their colleagues across the country, these teachers are looking beyond specific math skills appropriate for kindergartners or second graders. They are asking themselves what mathematical insights all people need to be useful, creative, and productive participants in a complex world.

Chapter 4

Counting on Community

There is increasing evidence that unless schools teach children to work collaboratively, they may lack the skills to function in a complex technological world.

Manufactured goods—from cars to crayons—are produced by teams of workers. The wax base of the crayons so popular with children, for example, is the product of a team of workers at Exxon Company, at their refinery in Baton Rouge, Louisiana. These workers know that because children are the consumers, the product must be of edible standards. When problems arise, everyone on the team—from executive engineer to hourly laborer—knows they are responsible for a part of the information and expertise needed to solve the problem.

The NCTM Standards advocate small group learning as a context that provides "a forum in which students ask questions, discuss ideas, make mistakes, learn to listen to others' ideas, offer constructive criticism, and summarize their discoveries in writing."

Collaborative math groups make math concepts accessible to all. Students talk about the problem they need to solve. They learn to listen to the different ideas and strategies of their partners and also how to articulate their own understanding so that teammates can know what they're thinking. They learn how to resolve differences of opinion, to help each other, and to teach each other. Too often, we expect students to listen but we don't teach them how. It is much easier to learn to listen in a group of four than in a group of 30. Groups of four certainly give students much more practice in learning to explain their own thinking and to listen to their peers' thinking, than do groups of 30.

Mathematics is well suited to small-group collaboration because there are problems with objective solutions, solutions that can be explained and demonstrated. This is not to say these solutions are reached by just one method. Students in small groups quickly learn there are different ways to reach solutions to math problems, discovering that they learn math by thinking, talking, listening, negotiating, and rethinking.

Some teachers who haven't tried collaborative groups in math worry that one of two things will happen. Either each member of the group will work independently on the problem, or one person will solve it while the other three sit and wait for the answer. One way experienced teachers encourage group members to work with each other is to assign different jobs to each group member, and then accept only one paper from the group. One person gets materials the group needs, another puts things away when work is finished. One group member is responsible for restating the problem the group is trying to solve. One person records the group's solution to the problem and records their thinking as well. When the whole class regroups, one person from each group acts as spokesperson, explaining their solution to the class. All the jobs are rotated within the group; every member learns to be responsible for supplies, for listening to others, and recording their thinking.

Students discover that they learn math by thinking, talking, listening, negotiating, and rethinking.

Forming Groups

Patricia Jiminez Weaver's combined class of seven and eight year olds in Tucson uses a deck of cards to choose partners. The deck has sets of four matching cards; for example, four cards with a five. All children choosing a "five" card go to the table labeled five. The two red fives are partners, and the two black fives are partners.

Some teachers employ a similar strategy for forming groups but alternate these groups with groups of the students' own choosing. They find that students are more cheerful about assigned groups when they know they also get to work with partners of their own choice.

Weaver is quick to admit that collaborative groups don't always cooperate. "Sometimes they spend a lot of time arguing," she says. Weaver stresses that children need plenty of opportunities to learn to cooperate. She points out that this is a skill to be taught—and learned—not a feeling that just appears spontaneously in children. "I role-play with a student partner how to get and use the supplies we need. Then I have children role-play the same situation in front of the class." Weaver also role-plays problem resolution with her students, giving them a model of how to work out difficulties.

Weaver admits that students are sometimes unhappy with their partners and ask to be switched. She reports that students invariably opt to stick it out. "They know that it isn't forever, that the groups will change. They also know that I believe it is important for us all to learn to accept differences among people."

An Inside-the-Classroom Look at Choosing Partners

Lynn Zolli feels it's important to provide choices for her third graders in San Francisco. After she introduces a new idea to the whole class, she might end the session with the question, "How many people would like to discuss this with someone else?" This offers children the possibility of working alone or with a partner. On other days she tells her students, "I'd like you to solve this problem with your group."

In Zolli's class, groups of four are chosen by lottery and remain constant for one month, when new groups form. Zolli gives her students plenty of opportunity to have free choice of partners, but during this free choice a rule remains in effect: you can't work with the same partner two days in a row. "If you don't change partners, you don't change roles," insists Zolli. "You need to work with people who don't think just like you do."

Lynn Zolli helps children see how to work cooperatively in a group. When groups of four are trying to figure out how to divide up large numbers of raisins, Vickie and Jeanne complain that Roger is messing up their count by eating the raisins. "He's eating the raisins. And all he does is argue with us," they complain to Ms. Zolli.

"Did you eat raisins?" asks Ms. Zolli. When Roger denies this, she advises the group, "It is your responsibility to tell Roger what to do. When you work in groups, you need to keep all members advised of what you need them to do."

Since groups record their work on just one record sheet, Zolli trains them to indicate how many copies they need of that record sheet when they turn it in at the end of the period. Students' work folders have pockets for "work in progress," "work finished," and "work to be copied." One member of a group of four will put the work the group finishes in the "work to be copied" pocket with the number "4" circled at the top, letting their teacher know they want four copies. She copies the work, keeping the original for her files, and returns the copies. Each group member then puts a copy in his or her "work finished" pocket. Zolli periodically goes through the "work finished" pockets, assessing and recording this work. Key here is the fact that it is the responsibility of these third graders to keep track of things.

On a day when Zolli has called the class to sit on the floor at the front of the room to listen to the story *17 Kings and 42 Elephants,* she gives the children free choice of partners for figuring out how to share 42 elephants among 17 kings. Four children scramble to get Eric to be their partner. Eric is regarded as a math whiz because as half a dozen children said in an interview about their attitudes about math, "Eric knows his facts really fast."

Andrew and David choose to work together. These two are both top math students and creative thinkers. David says that if he could change one thing about math it would be to "work in groups all the time. I like working with people. I don't care how many partners I have—one or three—I just would rather not work alone." Adam says that when the teacher tells the class to work alone he feels "kind of disappointed—because working in groups helps me learn about other people."

Roger asks Greg if he'd like to be his partner, thus disproving the worry that no one will choose the least able student as a partner. Greg is a mainstreamed child who has great difficulty in all school work. Although he enjoys discussing literature, he finds ways to avoid math much of the time. But he is enthusiastic when Roger asks him to collaborate. Roger talks Greg through much of the problem and when Roger gets stuck, Greg provides an offbeat solution that delights them—and their classmates.

By the time I had interviewed the children in this class about how they feel when Ms. Zolli asks them to work alone in math class, I'd been watching them and working with them for a month and I knew them pretty well, or thought I did. My question to students was open-ended: "When our teacher tells us to work alone in math I feel…" I thought I could predict whether most of these children preferred working alone or in groups. I was wrong about 70 percent of the time. I was startled to learn that six to one, boys preferred working in groups to working alone. In contrast, girls stood three to one in their preference for solitary work. I was surprised by the fact that among the boys, both the strongest and the weakest math students spoke out strongly in favor of group work. Among the girls, the strongest math students preferred to work alone.

Field Notes: Teacher-To-Teacher

When asked how they feel about working in groups, three boys saw two sides of reality rather than as a positioning of opposites. Mark, for example, replied, "When our teacher tells us to work in groups in math I feel good, because it's fun to work in groups. When our teacher tells us to work alone in math I feel smart, because you get to do it yourself." Roger, the boy who invited Greg to be his partner, responded that working in groups makes him feel "great because I get to help." For Roger, working alone is also great because "I get to think and nobody gives me answers." Mike was candid that he doesn't like working in groups because he has "to wait a lot for the other kids," but he doesn't like working alone either because he has "to work hard." When I persisted and asked, "Well, which would you rather do—work in a group or work alone?" Mike let me know he thought it was a stupid question. "I'd rather not do it at all. I only do it because I have to. I'd rather draw."

–SO

A variety of learning experiences helps children gain insight into their own best working styles.

My observations of and conversations with these children show me that the variety of learning experiences has provided these eight year olds with the opportunity to gain valuable insights into their own best working styles. They gained this insight because their teacher works hard at providing a flexible structure in her class, one that encourages both solitary and cooperative work, one that gives children room to make choices.

More Classroom Views

Ellen Thompson feels that teaching a first-second-third grade combination class in Colchester, Vermont, is ideal. "Third graders are the veterans; they train the first graders." Thompson designates group leaders, pointing out that it works very well to put first graders in charge. Thompson feels it's a mistake to allow the best writers to automatically assume the role of recorder. During the second half of the year, first graders take the lion's share of recording responsibility. "This pushes first graders to stretch themselves and it helps the other students, too," explains Thompson. "Students need to understand the material very well in order to be able to dictate it to the recorder."

In Rio Rancho, Penny Vincent reminds her third graders at Ernest Stapleton School throughout the day that they need to help and rely on each other. They are working on an art-related math project, and some students are much more adept with scissors than others. "If you're having trouble cutting," reminds Vincent, "ask someone at your table to help you." When a student asks Vincent, "Will you help me? I forget how to do it," Vincent responds, "Check with your group. Someone will help you." When Joey complains, "I'm not good at this," one of his tablemates both consoles and encourages him—and gets him back on track. As the math period nears the end, Vincent invites students to walk around the room and look at each other's work. "Notice how you all received the same instructions but you created very different results because people think differently. Let's enjoy all the variety we see here."

Before her fifth graders in Albuquerque write in their journals after a math class in which new concepts were introduced, Louise Nielsen tells them, "When I ask you to write about math, it is not a test. Let's communicate what we know before you write. Let's add to the classroom store of information by sharing our knowledge before you begin to write your own thoughts."

Nielsen emphasizes this community of knowledge by working hard at making sure that her classroom is not a place where students maneuver and manipulate to get her praise for their work. "We talk about the work in terms of mathematics, not in terms of good and bad," explains Nielsen. When Kris, who is working on a tessellation asks, "Ms. Nielsen, how's this?" Nielsen replies, "Is it a flip or a slide?" Another time she might deflect that question back to the student, asking, "What do you think?"

As she walks around the room looking at her students' work on tessellations, she asks repeatedly, "Did you do a flip or a slide?" She encourages students to become comfortable with using the precise vocabulary of the subject they are studying. Terms such as rhombus, horizontal, vertical, and rotation fill the air. Nielsen invites Maria to look at Kris's work and make comparisons of technique, "Do you see any similarities? any differences?"

Nielsen, who has been teaching for eight years, says her fifth graders chose the furniture arrangement of the classroom. "They chose to be in groups of three," says Nielsen. "So it's not conventional wisdom about cooperative grouping that's important to me, but honoring children's wishes. After all, I did ask for their opinions. So I can't ignore it."

Tips on Learning To Collaborate
- Groups are usually from two to five people.
- Heterogeneous groups are encouraged. Children work with team-mates who perceive problems in different ways, who contribute different insights and strategies.
- Each member of the group has an organizational responsibility: one may get the materials the group needs; one may remind the group of their task; one may write for the group.
- Each member of the group must be willing to help any group member who asks.
- The teacher is not to be consulted unless everyone in the group has the same question or problem. This is difficult—especially for the teacher—at first. But by enforcing this principle, the teacher convinces group members they must talk to one another.
- The teacher takes an active role, circulating from group to group, listening and nudging. She or he may become a member of a group and engage in the task as one of the group.
- The teacher provides time for students to come together as a whole class and listen to the findings of various groups.

To get her combined class of fourth and fifth graders in Lincoln, California, used to the idea of working together, Shirley Russell asked them to predict what they could do in one minute: how many times could they jump a rope and bounce a basketball, how many times did their heart beat, and so on. Russell emphasized that to get valid answers, each group of students needed a player, a timer, a counter, and a recorder. The group recorder wrote each group member's name on a record chart and also recorded each prediction. The timekeeper told the group when to start and when to stop. The counter told the recorder the correct count, and verified its entry on the chart.

Group members rotated jobs until everyone had done every activity. Then they discussed the results and formulated a conclusion, which the recorder wrote. This rotation gave students more data to work with—and ensured that everyone took a stab at writing about math. When the whole class came together at the end of the activity, a representative from each group shared his or her conclusions with the whole group.

Russell chose this activity because she wanted something with relatively "non-emotional" content for her students' introduction to collaborative grouping, something where there would not be comparisons of who "got" it and who didn't, who was smart and who wasn't. Russell wants her students to get their feet wet with recording observations of physical facts before they move on to more challenging activities that involve prior knowledge, talent, learning styles, and beliefs.

Groups Have Two Tasks

Collaborative groups have an academic problem to solve. They also have lots of interpersonal skills to develop.

Patricia Weaver interrupts math class to role-play an interpersonal problem, showing children how they might resolve such a problem. "Children need to practice these skills just as much as their math facts," she comments. Shirley Russell agrees. "We have to remember that it's hard for students to be nice to each other if they haven't had that experience themselves. We need to give them time, space, and opportunity to practice cooperation. If they have their noses in workbooks, they certainly aren't going to learn to listen to someone else's ideas."

Hour by hour, the configuration of learning changes in a classroom; children learn in whole group lessons, in small group sharing, and in individual investigation. It is as vital to remember that students need individual messing around time, individual quiet time, as well as time to learn to communicate their ideas to other people.

Forming New Partnerships

In Flemington, New Jersey, basic skills teacher (Title 1/Chapter 1) Glenn Coats, is struck by the profound changes he is witnessing in mathematics education. Coats accompanies ten-year-old Barbara into her regular math classroom. "As my role shifts, as I follow Barbara into her regular classroom instead of isolating her from her peers so she can work her way through a stack of skill drill worksheets, Barbara's role also changes in profound ways."

Barbara is carrying a few trays of base ten blocks. A child who confesses she used to hate math because she "didn't get it," Barbara enters her mainstream classroom on this day as expert consultant. The "regular" students immediately gather around Barbara, wanting to know about these unfamiliar materials she's carrying. Coats reports that they are as excited as if she'd brought a puppy or a snack into their classroom. And Barbara, a child who was formerly viewed as an "outsider" and "different," holds the secret of how to use these new materials.

Barbara is the only student who knows what the manipulatives are for—and how to use them. Being an expert informant is a new role for this child who often has difficulty with traditional paper-and-pencil mathematics. She is proud of her new function and is beginning to find her strengths through using manipulatives. Coats is finding her strengths as well. Instead of working with her in isolation, he observes Barbara's strengths and weaknesses in the "real" school world. This helps him plan ways to help her build on her strengths. At intervals, he works with the classroom teacher to plan lessons in which Barbara's experience with manipulatives can give her the opportunity to be a proficient and expert informant to her classmates.

"They were very interested in what I showed them," Barbara tells Mr. Coats later, recounting with pride her experience of being a teacher. "They wanted to learn what I already knew." Barbara comments later, "I like being a teacher."A child who was formerly weighed down by what she didn't know and by the belief that her brain "didn't work right," Barbara is no longer afraid to try new things. She and her teachers are planning together for another surprise. Barbara is confident that her fourth grade classmates will like to learn about chip trading. She is working hard at developing the expertise she knows is necessary to be able to teach them. Coats reflects that not only is Barbara gaining new confidence in her skills as she earns the respect of her peers, she is also introducing manipulative materials into the mainstream curriculum.

DIALOGUE

Here are some questions that you may want to ask yourself about your students' experiences with math:

Yes No

☐ ☐ Do all my students see themselves as good mathematicians?

☐ ☐ Do my students see math as involving a wide range of topics?

☐ ☐ Are my students developing a flexible repertoire of problem-solving strategies?

☐ ☐ Are my students able to communicate their problem-solving strategies to others? Do they talk and write about how they solve math problems?

☐ ☐ Do my students reflect on their work? Do they develop and use criteria to evaluate their performance?

☐ ☐ Do my students engage in mathematical thinking without a specific assignment?

☐ ☐ Are my students developing the attitudes of independent, self-motivated thinkers and problem solvers?

☐ ☐ Do my students welcome challenge in math? Are they they able to focus on math problems of increasing complexity for increasing lengths of time?

☐ ☐ Do my students recognize the importance of math in the world outside of school? Do they volunteer stories of math-in-action in the real world?

☐ ☐ Do my students see the beauty of mathematics and experience its power?

More of our answers move to the "yes" column as our students become involved in an active, problem-solving role rather than in a passive, acted-upon role. Active learning requires challenge, exploration, and give and take. Discussion with other students enhances active learning.

The Power and the Beauty

Think of mathematics the way gardener-philosopher Michael Pollan thinks about his garden when he says "a garden is never finished." Too often, the people who comment on educational policy and practice are not the people who closet themselves with a room full of eight year olds 182 days a year. Their ideal classrooms are neat and tidy. Their goals are sequenced. Teachers know that teaching and learning is not neat and tidy; it is messy, ambiguous, and contradictory. Twenty years in real classrooms has shown me that teachers need a good dose of what John Keats called *negative capability*—the ability to exist among uncertainties, mysteries, doubts. They need ever to resist that irritable reaching for fact and resolution.

Teachers know that teaching and learning is not neat and tidy; it is messy, ambiguous, and contradictory.

The classroom is an unhappy place for the perfectionist. Too much stands beyond our control. Again, Michael Pollan offers a nice metaphor in his book *Second Nature: A Gardener's Education* (1991), when he notes that "success in the garden is the moment in time, that week in June when the perennials unanimously bloom and the border jells, or those clarion days in September when the reds rest in the tomato patch—just before the black frost hits." Pollan confesses he still careens "from blunders of undercultivation to blunders of overcultivation."

Likewise, classroom success is transitory. "The blunders of undercultivation and overcultivation" are good metaphors of what it means to be a teacher. As Marilyn Burns warned an audience of California teachers, who had come together for three days of training in new ways to introduce multiplication to their students, "If you leave here feeling expert, you should worry about that." Burns cautions teachers that they need to see how new ideas look in their own classroom, and then time to reflect on what they see. "You can't think and teach at the same time. And you can't think about what it means until you've taught it and had some time to reflect on that teaching."

Pollan says of planting a maple tree, "To embark on a project that would outlast me, to plant a tree whose crown would never shade me but my children or, more likely, the children of strangers; tree planting is always a utopian enterprise, it seems to me, a wager on a future the planter doesn't necessarily expect to witness."

Poet-professor-farmer Wendell Berry says that trees on a farm are a sign of the farmer's "long-term good intentions toward the place." Isn't teaching similar?

Teaching, too, is a wager on the future. We teach for our students' children and their children; we teach as evidence of our "long-term good intentions."

In his introduction to the four-volume *The World of Mathematics* (1988), editor James R. Newman observes that an anthology is "a book of prejudice." He admits being bored by magic squares but captivated by probability. He prefers "geometry to algebra, physics to chemistry, logic to economics, the mathematics of infinity to the theory of numbers." Newman writes, "I have shunned topics, skimped some and shown great hospitality to others... I have felt at liberty to present the mathematics I like." If we can accept Newman's track and pursue the mathematics that intrigues and dazzles us, then our students will be the winners.

Every teacher feels a pang of guilt upon encountering Huckleberry Finn's declaration, "I had been to school... and could say the multiplication table up to 6 x 7 = 35, and I don't reckon I could ever get any further than that if I was to live forever. I don't take no stock in mathematics, anyway."

In *Archimedes' Revenge: The Challenge of the Unknown. The Joys and Perils of Mathematics* (1988), Paul Hoffman acknowledges that "By dipping into a handful of mathematical topics, you'll not learn everything that's important in mathematics," but more important, he thinks, you'll realize that mathematics is not cut and dry. It is full of surprises and mystery. "Number and shape are among humanity's oldest concerns, and yet much about them is still not understood." For example, no one knows "if there's an infinite number of perfect numbers, integers like 6 that are equal to the sum of all their divisors except, of course, the integer itself. The ancients knew of only four perfect numbers: 6, 28, 496, and 8,128. So far, 30 have been discovered."

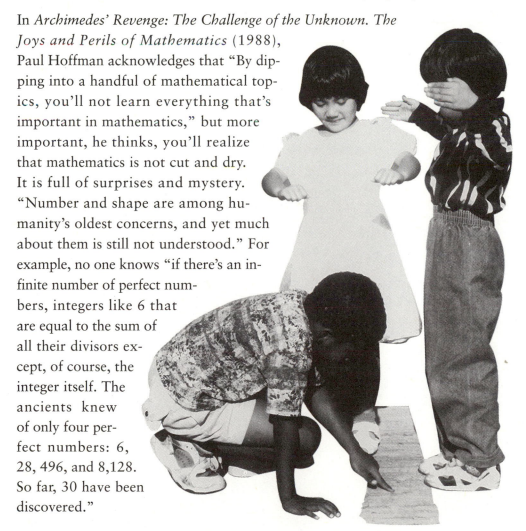

You are bringing many things to your students. You are teaching them to work collaboratively as well as independently; you are teaching them to talk with one another to discuss and define mathematical possibilities, to deal with uncertainty, to build mathematical theory. Students are learning that mathematics is much more than a series of numerical operations to be memorized. As they encounter mathematics in art, music, social studies, and literature, students are learning about the power and mystery of this thing called mathematics.

Professional Bibliography

Apelman, Maja and Julie King. *Exploring Everyday Math: Ideas for Students, Teachers, and Parents*. Portsmouth, New Hampshire: Heinemann, 1993. The ideas presented here help elementary-age students make connections between mathematics and their daily lives.

Axelson, Sharon. "Supermarket Challenge," *Arithmetic Teacher*, October 1992. Combining math and social studies, the article challenges students to use register tape receipts to classify, graph, and interpret information.

Baker, Ann and Johnny Baker. *Raps and Rhymes in Maths*. Portsmouth, New Hampshire: Heinemann, 1991. This is a collection of rhymes, riddles, and stories with mathematical themes for all grades.

Baker, Dave, Cheryl Semple and Tony Stead. *How Big Is the Moon?* Portsmouth, New Hampshire: Heinemann, 1990. This book provides sample elementary units that integrate math into the broader curriculum.

Baretta-Lorton, Mary. *Mathematics Their Way*. Menlo Park, California: Addison-Wesley, 1976. This is a highly influential activity-oriented math curriculum for primary grades.

Bridges, Lois. *Assessment: Continuous Learning*. Strategies for Teaching and Learning Professional Library, The Galef Institute. York, Maine: Stenhouse Publishers, 1995. See how authentic assessment invites teachers to find out what children know, how they can use what they know to learn, and what they can teach us. The author provides kidwatching and assessment forms that have been recommended by a variety of classroom teachers.

_____. *Creating Your Classroom Community.* Strategies for Teaching and Learning Professional Library, The Galef Institute. York, Maine: Stenhouse Publishers, 1995. Reading lofts, learning centers, student art, and more create an atmosphere where children want to learn.

Burns, Marilyn. *About Teaching Mathematics: A K-8 Resource.* White Plains, New York: Math Solutions/Cuisenaire Company, 1992. More than 240 classroom-tested problem-solving activities are surrounded by discussion about what is important in mathematics education in a changing world.

_____. "Helping Your Students Make Sense Out of Math," *Learning 88,* January 1988. Anecdotes from classrooms give valuable insight.

_____. *The Good Time Math Event Book.* Sunnyvale, California: Creative Publications, 1977. Seventy math activities organized by strands are presented here for elementary grades.

_____. *Math and Literature (K-3).* White Plains, New York: Math Solutions/Cuisenaire Company, 1992. The sample primary lessons connect a deep exploration of mathematics principles with children's picture books.

_____. *Math By All Means: Multiplication Grade 3.* White Plains, New York: Math Solutions/Cuisenaire Company, 1991. This five-week unit in multiplication is intended to replace standard textbook approaches.

_____. *Mathematics: With Manipulatives* (6 videos and teacher discussion guides). White Plains, New York: Cuisenaire Company, 1992. Techniques with pattern blocks, Cuisenaire rods, and color tiles are shown here. Also, *Mathematics: Teaching for Understanding*—3 videos showing the NCTM Standards implemented in elementary classroom lessons.

Burns, Marilyn, Cathy Humphreys and Bonnie Tank. *A Collection of Math Lessons.* White Plains, New York: Math Solutions/Cuisenaire Company, 1988. A series of three books presents math lessons through classroom vignettes. Primary, elementary, and middle school.

Burrows, Roger. *Images 2: The Ultimate Coloring Experience.* Philadelphia: Running Press, 1992. Coloring can be fun and challenging at all ages.

California State Department of Education. *The Changing Mathematics Curriculum: A Booklet for Parents.* Sacramento: California State Department of Education, 1989. This booklet explains to parents why mathematics teaching needs to change.

_____. *Mathematics: Model Curriculum Guide, K-8.* Sacramento: California State Department of Education, 1987. The guide spells out expectations in mathematical thinking by grade level.

_____. *A Question of Thinking: A First Look at Students' Performance on Open-ended Questions in Mathematics.* Sacramento: California State Department of Education, 1989. You'll find examples of how new tests probe children's mathematical understanding.

Confer, Chris. *Math By All Means: Geometry Grades 1-2.* White Plains, New York: Math Solutions/Cuisenaire Company, 1994. This Marilyn Burns replacement unit shows teachers how to help children construct their own understanding of the properties of shapes.

Coombs, Betty and Jennifer Travis. *Explorations.* Don Mills, Ontario: Addison-Wesley, 1987. The authors present an activity-based primary math program. Using manipulatives, the program is based on problem solving and getting children talking about their thinking.

Cuisenaire Company of America. *Learning With...Teacher Guides.* White Plains, New York: Cuisenaire Company, 1992–1995. Cuisenaire offers these guides to help teachers get started with manipulatives.

Dale Seymour. *Tessellation Winners: The First Contest.* Palo Alto, California: Dale Seymour Publications, 1991. Student creations from primary through high school show how tessellations interweave art, geometry, and design.

Duckworth, Eleanor. *The Having of Wonderful Ideas and Other Essays on Teaching and Learning.* New York: Teachers College Press, 1987. Here is an inspiring account of teachers and children learning to value thinking.

Eichelberger, Barbara and Connie Larson. *Constructions for Children: Projects in Design Technology.* Palo Alto, California: Dale Seymour Publications, 1993. This resource features real-world problem-solving activities using everyday materials.

Elementary Science Study. *ESS Tangram Cards, Set I, Set II, Set III.* Palo Alto, California: Dale Seymour Publications, 1968, 1988. The activities enhance spatial problem-solving skills.

_____. *Teacher Guides.* Nashua, New Hampshire: Delta Education, 1960s–70s. Thirty-six of the original ESS guides provide helpful examples integrating mathematics and science.

_____. *Musical Instrument Recipe Book.* Nashua, New Hampshire: Delta Education, 1970. Learn to make guitars out of bleach bottles and fish line, as well as other musical instruments with this "how to" book.

EQUALS staff. *Assessment Alternatives in Mathematics.* Berkeley: Lawrence Hall of Science/University of California, 1989. This overview of assessment techniques includes portfolios, writing, and interviews that promote learning for primary through high school.

Erickson, Tim. *Get It Together: Math Problems for Groups*. Berkeley: Lawrence Hall of Science/University of California, 1989. Here is a collection of math problems for groups, not individuals, to solve together. Elementary through high school.

Gardner, Howard. *Frames of Mind: The Theory of Multiple Intelligences*. New York: Basic Books, 1983. Gardner makes the reader aware of the many facets of intelligence.

Garland, Trudi Hammel. *Fascinating Fibonaccis: Mystery and Magic in Numbers*. Palo Alto, California: Dale Seymour Publications, 1987. This book takes students—and their teachers—into an astounding world of number patterns.

Giganti, Paul, Jr. and Mary Jo Cittadino. "The Art of Tessellation," *Arithmetic Teacher*, March 1990. This article gets students started with tessellations and explains the "nibble technique."

Greene, Maxine. *Landscapes of Learning*. New York: Teachers College, 1978. This book is a classic clarion call for thoughtful teaching.

Griffiths, Rachel and Margaret Clyne. *Books You Can Count On: Linking Mathematics and Literature*. Portsmouth, New Hampshire: Heinemann, 1991. You'll find out how to use primary and elementary picture books as a springboard for math activities.

Hawkins, David. *The Informed Vision*. New York: Agathon/Schocken, 1974. Hawkins's vision celebrates student thinking.

Heller, Paul G. *Drama as a Way of Knowing*. Strategies for Teaching and Learning Professional Library, The Galef Institute. York, Maine: Stenhouse Publishers, 1995. Learn how improvisation, pantomime, script writing, research, and acting are tools for learning.

Hilts, Philip. *Scientific Temperaments: Three Lives in Contemporary Science*. New York: Touchstone/Simon & Schuster, 1982. This is a readable, funny account of how scientists behave in the real world.

Hoffman, Paul. *Archimedes' Revenge: The Challenge of the Unknown. The Joys and Perils of Mathematics*. New York: W. W. Norton, 1988. Full of practical questions as well as engaging fancies, the book demonstrates the human side of mathematics.

Hofstadter, Douglas. *Metamagical Themes: Questions for the Essence of Mind and Pattern*. New York: Basic Books, 1985. Don't let the title scare you. This book contains some wonderfully playful puzzlers to inspire teachers to search for patterns—and to play with words and numbers.

Holt, John. *How Children Fail*. New York: Dell, 1964. This very readable classic shows how traditional arithmetic teaching promotes failure. Holt also provides concrete examples of how to help children learn.

_____. *Learning All the Time*. Reading, Massachusetts: Addison-Wesley, 1989. Classroom anecdotes provoke teachers to take a new look at their students.

Hope, Jack. *Mental Math in the Primary Grades*. Palo Alto, California: Dale Seymour Publications, 1988. Thirty-six lessons develop understanding of the base ten system through patterns.

Hyde, Arthur A. and Pamela R. Hyde. *Mathwise: Teaching Mathematical Thinking and Problem Solving*. Portsmouth, New Hampshire: Heinemann, 1991. Ten strategies help primary and elementary students develop their mathematical thinking—and share it through discussion, reading, and writing.

Jacobs, Harold R. *Mathematics: A Human Endeavor*. San Francisco: W. H. Freeman, 1982. This college math text helps students see the beauty and playfulness of math. The text is also used in teacher in-service courses.

Kamii, Constance. *Young Children Reinvent Arithmetic*. New York: Teachers College Press, 1985. *Young Children Continue To Reinvent Arithmetic—2nd Grade*. New York: Teachers College Press, 1989. Kamii offers insightful studies of the resources children bring to their understanding of mathematics.

Kaye, Peggy. *Games for Learning*. New York: Farrar Straus Giroux, 1991. These games encourage primary-age children to think—appropriate for school and home. Also see her *Games for Math*.

Krause, Marina. *Multicultural Mathematics Materials*. Reston, Virginia: National Council of Teachers of Mathematics, 1990. Projects range from ancient Egyptian games to tangrams to the geometry of Hopi pottery.

Mathematical Sciences Education Board/National Research Council. *Measuring Up: Prototypes for Mathematics Assessment*. Washington, DC: National Academy Press, 1993. Thirteen prototype assessment tasks show the meaning of a standards-based mathematical education at the fourth grade level.

National Council for the Social Studies. Theme Issue: "Social Mathematics Shapes Our View of the World." *Social Studies and the Young Learner*, September-October 1993. The suggested activities link social studies and mathematical content, processes, and purposes.

National Council of Teachers of Mathematics. *Curriculum and Evaluation Standards for School Mathematics*. Reston, Virginia: NCTM, 1989.

The NCTM Standards created goals for K-12 mathematics instruction that have been endorsed by such diverse groups as the Institute of Electrical and Electronics Engineers and the American Bankers Association. These groups have recognized that American students will need a deep understanding of mathematics to compete in a technological world.

_____.Focus Issue: "Spatial Sense." *Arithmetic Teacher,* February 1990. This issue highlights spatial understandings necessary for interpreting, understanding, and appreciating our geometric world.

National Research Council. *Everybody Counts.* Washington, DC: National Academy Press, 1989. This very readable report examines mathematics education as all one system. From kindergarten through graduate school, it both identifies problems and recommends a future course for mathematics.

National Sciences Education Board/National Research Council. *Counting on You.* Washington, DC: National Academy Press, 1991. *Counting on You* describes the basic issues in mathematics education and makes recommendations.

Newman, James R., ed. *The World of Mathematics.* Redmond, Washington: Tempus Books/Microsoft Press, 1988. This book is a comprehensive collection of classic essays on mathematics.

Ohanian, Susan. *Dates with the Greats: Being an Assembly of Anecdotes Embracing History, Literature, Science, Mathematics, Sports, Art, Music, and Popular Culture Collected for a Teacher's Pleasure and To Enrich and Enlighten the Lives of Children.* Chicago: Macmillan/McGraw-Hill, 1992. Daily stories can make numbers in your classroom fascinating.

_____. *Garbage Pizza, Patchwork Quilts, and Math Magic: Stories About Teachers Who Love To Teach and Children Who Love To Learn.* New York: W. H. Freeman, 1992. Here's a cross-country look inside classrooms that make the NCTM Standards come alive. Strategies for parental involvement are included.

_____. "How To Measure a Pig and Other Math Secrets," *Learning 86,* October 1986. The article takes an inside-the-classroom look at children's measurement strategies.

_____. "Record-Setting Math," *Learning 90,* May-June 1990. Find out how the *Guinness Book of World Records* (Sterling Publishing annual) can spur students to find fascinating numbers in the world they live in.

Page, Nick. *Music as a Way of Knowing.* Strategies for Teaching and Learning Professional Library, The Galef Institute. York, Maine: Stenhouse Publishers, 1995. The rhythm of music, singing, and building instruments can help us learn about ourselves, cultures, math, building community, and self-worth.

Pollan, Michael. *Second Nature: A Gardener's Education*. New York: Atlantic Monthly Press, 1991. Find out what gardening, education, and mathematics have in common.

Rectanus, Cheryl. *Math By All Means: Geometry Grades 3-4*. White Plains, New York: Math Solutions/Cuisenaire Company, 1994. This five-week Marilyn Burns replacement unit shows teachers how to help children explore geometric concepts by sorting, classifying, drawing, describing, combining, and modeling shapes.

Reimer, Luetta and Wilbert Reimer. *Mathematicians Are People, Too: Stories from the Lives of Great Mathematicians*. Palo Alto, California: Dale Seymour Publications, 1990. Fifteen stories tell about famous mathematicians and their appreciation of pattern.

Resnick, Lauren. *Education and Learning To Think*. Washington, DC: National Academy Press, 1987. Resnick provides a pedagogical base that helps readers understand the changes taking place in mathematics and other curriculums.

Russell, Susan Jo and Rebecca Corwin. *Sorting: Groups and Graphs. Statistics: The Shape of the Data*. Used Numbers: Real Data in the Classroom Series. Palo Alto, California: Dale Seymour Publications, 1990. These books prepare students to live in an information-rich world. Students are actively involved in collecting, organizing, and interpreting real-world data. Other titles in the series include *Counting: Ourselves and Our Families; Measuring: From Paces to Feet; Statistics: Middles, Means, and In-Betweens*; and *Statistics: Prediction and Sampling*.

Schon, Donald. *The Reflective Practitioner*. New York: Basic Books, 1983. Already a classic, Schon lays groundwork for what it means to be an actively reflective professional.

Steen, Lynn Arthur, ed. *On the Shoulders of Giants: New Approaches to Numeracy*. Washington, DC: National Academy Press, 1990. Steen issues a convincing call for math reform.

Stenmark, Jean Kerr, Virginia Thompson and Ruth Cossey. *Family Math*. Berkeley: Lawrence Hall of Science/University of California, 1986. This resource of 90 plus activities helps teachers and parents promote student enthusiasm for mathematics. Available in Spanish. Ages five to thirteen.

Tierney, Bob. "What's in a Receipt?" *Learning 88*, January 1988. Students make predictions about shoppers from studying grocery receipts.

Toufexis, Anastasia. "Exploring the Tea Bag Factor," *Time*, August 1991. The article discusses the importance of spatial intelligence as it relates to surviving captivity.

Trafton, Paul and Albert Shulte, eds. *New Directions for Elementary School Mathematics: 1989 Yearbook*. Reston, Virginia: National Council of Teachers of Mathematics, 1989. The broad components of change in elementary school mathematics are addressed through samples of student work.

U.S. Department of Labor. *What Work Requires of Schools: A SCANS Report for America 2000*. Washington, DC: U.S. Department of Labor, 1991. Corporate America lists five workplace competencies needed for jobs in the 21st century.

Wexler-Sherman, Carey, Howard Gardner and David Henry Feldman. "A Pluralistic View of Early Assessment: The Project Spectrum Approach," *Theory Into Practice*, Winter 1988. The article looks at the variety of preferred learning modes of preschoolers.

Whitin, David, Heidi Mills and Timothy O'Keefe. *Living and Learning Mathematics: Stories and Strategies for Supporting Mathematical Literacy*. Portsmouth, New Hampshire: Heinemann, 1990. This book provides an inside look at the mathematical strategies of primary-age children.

Whitin, David and Sandra Wilde. *Read Any Good Math Lately? Children's Books for Mathematical Learning, K-6*. Portsmouth, New Hampshire: Heinemann, 1992. Each of twelve chapters focuses on a math topic or concept, helping teachers to see how math can be integrated with literature.

Wiggins, Grant. *Assessing Student Performance*. San Francisco, California: Jossey-Bass, 1994. This book provides examples that ground a child-centered philosophy in specific pedagogy.

_____. "The Futility of Trying To Teach Everything of Importance," *Educational Leadership*, November 1989. Already a classic, this essay is in everyone's bibliography.

Willoughby, Stephen S. *Mathematics Education for a Changing World*. Alexandria, Virginia: Association for Supervision and Curriculum Development, 1990. Willoughby works at providing practical classroom applications of the NCTM Standards.

Zaslavsky, Claudia. "Symmetry in American Folk Art," *Arithmetic Teacher*, September 1990. Find out about the mathematics of quilts.

Children's Bibliography

Adams, Barbara Johnson. *The Go-Around Dollar*. New York: Four Winds Press, 1992. This explanation of the money cycle includes such facts as it takes 490 one-dollar bills to make one pound. Ages eight to twelve.

Aker, Suzanne. *What Comes in 2s, 3s, and 4s?* New York: Simon and Schuster, 1990. Children see multiplication in real life. Ages six to nine.

Anno, Mitsumasa. *Anno's Counting House*. New York: Philomel, 1982. *Anno's Magic Hat Tricks*. New York: Philomel, 1984. *Anno's Mysterious Multiplying Jar*. New York: Philomel, 1983. These imaginative works help children see the beauty and power of mathematics. Ages five to twelve.

Bang, Molly. *Ten, Nine, Eight*. New York: Greenwillow, 1983. This short book teaches kids counting backwards. Ages five and six.

Baum, Arline and Joseph Baum. *Opt: An Illusionary Tale*. New York: Puffin, 1987. The mathematics of optical illusions and measurement are revealed. Ages six to twelve.

Birch, David. *The King's Chessboard*. New York: Dial, 1988. A wise man outsmarts a vain king when he is offered a reward—and reveals the astounding power of doubling. Ages seven to twelve.

Burns, Marilyn. *The I Hate Mathematics! Book*. Boston: Little, Brown, 1975. *The Book of Think*. Boston: Little, Brown, 1976. *Math for Smarty Pants*. Boston: Little, Brown, 1982. These classics in the Brown Paper

School Book series continue to be popular with children and teachers. Ages nine to fourteen.

_____. *The $1.00 Word Riddle Book*. White Plains, New York: Math Solutions/Cuisenaire Company, 1990. This book of riddles and puzzles challenges children to figure out what words add up to $1.00 when a = $.01, b = $.02, and on through z = $.26. Ages eight to fourteen.

Burrows, Roger. *Images 2: The Ultimate Coloring Experience*. Philadelphia: Running Press, 1992. Students find patterns and create unique art. Ages eight to thirteen.

Chwast, Seymour. *The 12 Circus Rings*. Boston: Harcourt Brace, 1993. Based on the structure of the "Twelve Days of Christmas," this book engages children in exciting number exploration; counting, adding, multiplying, and discovering patterns. All ages.

Clement, Ron. *Counting on Frank*. Milwaukee, Wisconsin: Gareth Stevens, 1991. This zany account of a boy who is a measuring maniac will cause readers of all ages to take a new look at everything from ball-point pens to growing peas. All ages.

Connell, David and Jim Thurman. *Mathnet Casebook* Series. New York: Children's Television Workshop/W. H. Freeman, 1993. The series is based on the television show. Ages nine to twelve.

Crews, Donald. *Ten Black Dots*. New York: Henry Holt, 1988. A Liberian folktale inspires consideration of patterns and factors. Ages six to eight.

Ernst, Lisa Campbell and Lee Ernst. *The Tangram Magician*. New York: Abrams, 1990. This story tells the tale of the tangram puzzle. Ages five to twelve.

Geringer, Laura. *A Three Hat Day*. Illustrated by Arnold Lobel. New York: Harper, 1985. The story of a man with several hats leads to an investigation of permutations. Ages six to ten.

Giganti, Paul, Jr. *Each Orange Had 8 Slices: A Counting Book*. Illustrated by Donald Crews. New York: Greenwillow, 1992. This original counting book is available in big book format. Ages five to eight.

Hertzberg, Hendrik. *One Million*. New York: Simon and Schuster, 1993. Written for adults, children love seeing what one million really looks like in the pages of *One Million*. There are 5,000 dots to a page. All ages.

Hulme, Joy. *Sea Squares*. New York: Hyperion, 1991. *Sea Squares* focuses on making predictions, squaring numbers from one to ten, and geometric relationships. Ages six to eight.

Hurwitz, Johanna. *Tough-Luck Karen*. New York: Beach Tree, 1991. A thirteen year old questions the relevance of math in her life. Ages ten to thirteen.

Hutchins, Pat. *The Doorbell Rang*. New York: Greenwillow, 1986. This story of cookies can be used to introduce division. It is available in big book format. Ages six to eight.

_____. *1 Hunter*. New York: Mulberry, 1982. Challenge students to figure out how many animals the hunter missed. Ages five to eight.

Juster, Norman. *The Phantom Tollbooth*. New York: Random House, 1961. Juster highlights the relationship between common and decimal fractions—and the meaning of statistics—when the hero meets half a child, the result of the average family having 2.58 children. Ages ten to thirteen.

Lakford, Mary D. *Hopscotch Around the World*. New York: William Morrow, 1992. Readers gain a sense of cultural link to numbers. Ages eight to twelve.

Leedy, Loreen. *The Monster Money Book*. New York: Holiday House, 1992. This is a fictional account of a club deciding what to do with $54 in their treasury. Ages seven to nine.

Lewis, Brenda Ralph. *Coins and Currency*. New York: Random House, 1993. Here's a great history of money and how it is made (and forged). Ages nine and up.

Maestro, Betsy. *The Story of Money*. New York: Clarion, 1993. Maestro provides a cross-cultural history of the modern monetary system. Ages eight to fourteen.

Mahy, Margaret. *17 Kings and 42 Elephants*. New York: Dial, 1987. Mahy's wonderful language can provoke a poster about equal sharing. Ages seven to nine.

Markle, Sandra. *Math Mini-Mysteries*. New York: Atheneum, 1993. Discover how to use math for everything from checking if the wind is right for kite-flying to measuring acid rain. You'll learn how math made it possible to carve the faces of four presidents on Mount Rushmore. Ages eight to thirteen.

Mathews, Louise. *Bunches and Bunches of Bunnies*. New York: Scholastic, 1978. This book offers a rhyming introduction to squares 1 x 1 to 12 x 12. It is also available in big book format. Ages eight to twelve.

Matthews, Peter. *The Guinness Book of Records*. New York: Facts on File, annual. Students will be fascinated and intrigued by these irresistible and impossible numbers. Ages nine to fourteen.

McCarthy, Patricia. *Ocean Parade*. New York: Dial, 1990. This counting book inspires deeper mathematical thinking. Ages five to eight.

McLaughlin, Molly. *Earthworms, Dirt, and Rotten Leaves*. New York: Avon, 1990. Irresistible questions (and answers) about earthworms encourage students to look carefully at the world around them.

Morozumi, Atsuko. *One Gorilla*. New York: Farrar, Straus and Giroux, 1990. This prize-winning counting book poses the problem of figuring out how many things the narrator loves. Ages five to eight.

Munsch, Robert. *Moira's Birthday*. Toronto, Canada: Annick Press, 1987. There are zany results when hundreds of children arrive for a birthday party and Moira has to figure out how to feed them. Ages five to eight.

Myller, Rolf. *How Big Is a Foot?* New York: Dell, 1992. The royal court gets into a snafu involving measurement. Ages seven to nine.

Paul, Ann Whitford. *Eight Hands Round*. New York: Harper, 1991. This patchwork alphabet book initiates the investigation of metaphor and geometric patterns. Ages seven to twelve.

Pinczes, Elinor. *One Hundred Hungry Ants*. Boston: Houghton Mifflin, 1993. Here are different ways to divide 100—in rhyme. Ages six to ten.

Polacco, Patricia. *The Keeping Quilt*. New York: Simon and Schuster, 1988. This beautiful book explores quilts and family traditions. All ages.

Reid, Margarette. *The Button Box*. New York: Dutton, 1990. Children learn about classification through a classroom button collection. Ages five and six.

Schwartz, Alvin. *10 Copycats in a Boat*. New York: Harper, 1980. Here's a classic riddle book for children ages six to nine.

Schwartz, David. *How Much Is a Million?* Also, *If You Made a Million*. New York: Lothrop, 1989. Concepts of million, billion, and trillion are explained using child-appealing images. Ages five to ten.

Thurber, James. *Many Moons*. Boston: Harcourt Brace, 1944. A Caldecott winner, this book presents intriguing problem solving. Ages eight to eleven.

Tompert, Ann. *Grandfather Tang's Story*. New York: Crown, 1990. This is a tangram story for children ages five to twelve.

Viorst, Judith. *Alexander, Who Used To Be Rich Last Sunday*. New York: Atheneum, 1978. Students will get practice with mental calculations. The story is also available in Spanish. Ages eight to ten.

Wyatt, Elaine and Stan Hinden. *The Money Book: A Smart Kid's Guide to Savvy Savings and Spending*. New York: Tambourine, 1991. Rooted in a real-world interest of children, this book offers practical information and advice. Ages eight to twelve.

Professional Associations and Publications

The American Alliance for Health, Physical Education, Recreation, and Dance (AAHPERD)
Journal of Physical Education, Recreation, and Dance
1900 Association Drive
Reston, Virginia 22091

American Alliance for Theater and Education (AATE)
AATE Newsletter
c/o Arizona State University Theater Department
Box 873411
Tempe, Arizona 85287

American Association for the Advancement of Science (AAAS)
Science Magazine
1333 H Street NW
Washington, DC 20005

American Association of Colleges for Teacher Education (AACTE)
AACTE Briefs
1 DuPont Circle NW, Suite 610
Washington, DC 20036

American Association of School Administrators (AASA)
The School Administrator
1801 North Moore Street
Arlington, Virginia 22209

Association for Childhood Education International (ACEI)
Childhood Education: Infancy Through Early Adolescence
11141 Georgia Avenue, Suite 200
Wheaton, Maryland 20902

Association for Supervision and Curriculum Development (ASCD)
Educational Leadership
1250 North Pitt Street
Alexandria, Virginia 22314

The Council for Exceptional Children (CEC)
Teaching Exceptional Children
1920 Association Drive
Reston, Virginia 22091

Education Theater Association (ETA)
Dramatics
3368 Central Parkway
Cincinnati, Ohio 45225

International Reading Association (IRA)
The Reading Teacher
800 Barksdale Road
Newark, Delaware 19714

Music Educators National Conference (MENC)
Music Educators Journal
1806 Robert Fulton Drive
Reston, Virginia 22091

National Art Education Association (NAEA)
Art Education
1916 Association Drive
Reston, Virginia 22091

National Association for the Education of
Young Children (NAEYC)
Young Children
1509 16th Street NW
Washington, DC 20036

National Association of Elementary School Principals (NAESP)
Communicator
1615 Duke Street
Alexandria, Virginia 22314

National Center for Restructuring Education, Schools,
and Teaching (NCREST)
Resources for Restructuring
P.O. Box 110
Teachers College, Columbia University
New York, New York 10027

National Council for the Social Studies (NCSS)
Social Education
Social Studies and the Young Learner
3501 Newark Street NW
Washington, DC 20016

National Council of Supervisors of Mathematics (NCSM)
NCSM Newsletter Leadership in Mathematics Education
P.O. Box 10667
Golden, Colorado 80401

National Council of Teachers of English (NCTE)
Language Arts
Primary Voices K-6
1111 Kenyon Road
Urbana, Illinois 61801

National Council of Teachers of Mathematics (NCTM)
Arithmetic Teacher
Teaching Children Mathematics
1906 Association Drive
Reston, Virginia 22091

National Dance Association (NDA)
Spotlight on Dance
1900 Association Drive
Reston, Virginia 22091

National Science Teachers Association (NSTA)
Science and Children
Science for Children: Resources for Teachers
1840 Wilson Boulevard
Arlington, Virginia 22201

Phi Delta Kappa
Phi Delta Kappan
408 North Union
Bloomington, Indiana 47402

Society for Research in Music Education
Journal for Research in Music Education
c/o Music Educators National Conference
1806 Robert Fulton Drive
Reston, Virginia 22091

The Southern Poverty Law Center
Teaching Tolerance
400 Washington Avenue
Montgomery, Alabama 36104

Teachers of English to Speakers of Other Languages (TESOL)
TESOL Newsletter
1600 Cameron Street, Suite 300
Alexandria, Virginia 22314

Other titles in the
Strategies for Teaching and Learning Professional Library

Administrators Supporting School Change
Robert Wortman
1-57110-047-4   paperback

In this fascinating personal account of how a principal can make a difference in the lives of all he touches through his work, noted principal Bob Wortman outlines his own strategies for creating a positive learning environment where everyone feels valued, respected, and can focus on the business of learning.

Fostering a successful school community demands more than a vision and a philosophy. A successful school administrator needs to know how to maintain positive relationships with all members of the school community—parents, students, and teachers. Classroom teachers, site and district administrators, parents, and policymakers will be interested in Bob's mission to create a schoolwide learning community that includes not only the people in the classrooms, but the support personnel, the families, and the community at large.

Assessment Continuous Learning
Lois Bridges
1-57110-048-2   paperback

Effective teaching begins with knowing your students, and assessment is a learning tool that enables you to know them. In this book Lois Bridges gives you a wide range of teacher-developed kidwatching and assessment forms to show different ways you can reflect on children's thinking and work. She offers developmental checklists, student and child interview suggestions, guidelines for using portfolios in your classroom, rubrics, and self-evaluation profiles. Also included are Dialogues that invite reflection, Shoptalks that offer lively reviews of the best and latest professional literature, and Teacher-To-Teacher Field Notes offering tips and experiences from practicing educators.

Lois identifies five perspectives on assessment—monitoring, observing, interacting, analyzing, and reporting—to think about when designing your own assessments. As you continuously evaluate and monitor your students' learning using a variety of assessment tools, you can design instruction and create curriculum that will stretch your students' knowledge and expand their learning worlds.

Creating Your Classroom **Community**
Lois Bridges
1-57110-049-0   paperback

What do you remember of your own elementary schooling experiences? Chances are the teachers you recall are those who really knew and cared for you as an unique individual with special interests, needs, and experiences. Now, as a teacher with your own classroom and students to care for, you'll want to create a classroom environment that supports each student as an individual while drawing the class together as a thriving learning community.

Lois Bridges offers you the basics of effective elementary school teaching: how to construct a curriculum that focuses not only on what you will teach but how you will teach and evaluate it; how to build a sense of community and responsibility among your students; and how to organize your classroom to support learning and to draw on learning resources from parents and the larger community beyond school.

Drama as a Way of Knowing
Paul G. Heller
1-57110-050-4   paperback

Paul Heller is an experienced teacher, playwright, and producer who is passionate about communicating through language, drama, and music. In this engaging book he shows you how to use drama as an effective part of all classroom learning. While making it clear you don't need previous dramatic training or experience, he presents the nuts and bolts of pantomime and improvisation, of writing and acting scenes, even creating and presenting large-scale productions.

Through his Ten-Step Process in which you, the teacher, are the director, he shows what you should do to guide your students through rewarding dramatic experiences. You will see that drama is a wonderful learning tool that enables students to explore multiple dimensions of their thinking and understanding. And not only is drama academically rewarding and beneficial, it's great fun as well!

Music as a Way of Knowing
Nick Page
1-57110-052-0   paperback

Nick Page loves to make and share music with his students, and it's likely that you will too by the time you've finished his passionate, thought-provoking book. You will also have developed a new understanding of and appreciation for the role music can play in supporting learners.

Rich with ideas on how to use music in the classroom, *Music as a Way of Knowing* will appeal especially to classroom teachers who are not musicians, but who enjoy and learn from music and want to use it with their students. Nick provides simple instructions for writing songs, using music to support learning across the curriculum, teaching singing effectively, and identifying good songs to use in the classroom.

He assures you that with time, all students can sing well. And once you've read this book, you'll have the confidence to trust yourself and your students to sing and learn well through the joy and power of music.